In Prayer
St. Michael, the Archangel

March 8, 1989 ... Here is Saint Michael:

✠ I, Saint Michael, pray without cease for this evil generation. Pray child, and obey the Lord; praise the Lord for the outpouring of His Spirit among you all.

St. Michael, thank you,

Peace to you

Photo: Courtesy of Black Rock College, Dublin, Ireland. Sculptured in Sussex Oak by Claire Sheridan.

True Life in God

Vassula

Volume Nine
(Notebook 79 - Notebook 87:18)

Original Handwriting Edition

Published by

Trinitas™

Declaration

The decree of the Congregation for the Doctrine of the Faith, A.A.S. 58, 1186 (approved by Pope Paul VI on October 14, 1966) states that the Nihil Obstat and Imprimatur are no longer required on publications that deal with private revelations, provided they contain nothing contrary to faith and morals.

The publisher wishes to manifest unconditional submission to the final and official judgment of the Magisterium of the Church.

True Life in God
Vassula
Volume Nine (Notebook 79 - Notebook 87:18)

Published by
Trinitas™

P.O. Box 475
Independence, Missouri, USA 64051-0475
Phone (816) 254-4489
FAX (816) 254-1469

ISBN: 1-883225-20-5

For further information direct all inquiries to Trinitas.

Cover photo: from Agamian Portrait, courtesy of Holy Shroud Guild.
Printed in United States of America.

Also available in Spanish, French, Italian, German, Croatian, Bulgarian, Mexican, Greek, Danish, Russian, Portuguese, Japanese, and other languages. For information contact Trinitas.

Table of Contents

The "Blossoming" of the Sacred Heart of Jesus in *True Life in God*

Jesus Christ is our perfect Teacher. He knows best how to reach the minds and hearts He Himself created. The following volume of messages offers further evidence that He has been painstakingly revealing to us a mystery so awesome that it has taken several millennia to make it truly accessible to all His children. Any attempt to summarize how He has been unveiling the "inexhaustible treasures" of His Sacred Heart would be miserably inadequate. Some who have been close to the messages have gained recent insights as part of the fruit of the presentations and tour of the U.S.A. and Canada in the Fall of 1996 and January of 1997. These insights will resonate with those whose hearts have been touched beyond words by reading and praying what Jesus calls His "Love Hymn from Heaven."

Vassula Ryden emphasizes in her presentations that God wants us to love Him but that we cannot do so unless we first <u>know</u> Him. He taught Vassula that in order to get to know Him we have to <u>approach</u> Him. In a message of April 1995 to the United States, Jesus says:

> **learn to glorify the Father and love Him so that the Father and I make Our home with you...**

How then has Jesus been inviting us to approach the Holy Trinity in this era of unprecedented materialism and secular rationalism?

Vassula points out that in the messages she has been receiving since 1985, Jesus introduces major themes and then revisits them in different words at deeper levels so that otherwise incomprehensible mysteries come within everyone's grasp. Some of these are the Holy Trinity, the Gifts of the Holy Spirit, the Immaculate Heart of Mary, the Church as the Body of Christ and its revival on the foundations of His "Primitive Church."

Those who have savored the exquisite teachings on these mysteries throughout the first eight volumes and *My Angel Daniel—Early Dawn of True Life in God* will be struck—as was Vassula herself—to realize in retrospect how the Lord was all along preparing us for these latest messages on the Seven Gifts of the Holy Spirit and the role of Mary, Mother of God in Our Father's plan of salvation.

This ninth volume (of the original handwriting edition) culminates in a precious "crown jewel" of a message given on the day of the eleventh anniversary of the beginning of the *True Life in God* messages. The richness of this very recent teaching astounded Father Michael O'Carroll,

Vassula's spiritual advisor, in whose priesthood the Sacred Heart of Jesus has always played a special role.

It was a privilege to witness Father Michael's grateful reaction when he first read this "Sacred Heart" message. Then a short time later, after Father began to share in his talks his own personal reflections on the Sacred Heart, Jesus graced him with a personal message. Vassula received this during the latter days of an 18-city speaking tour throughout the U.S.:

> **...tell your counsellor that "I am filled with joy that at last your thoughts on My Sacred Heart are blossoming in your mouth. I know that you always considered My Heart as Heaven, but had not so many opportunities to expose My Heart as now....I have chosen you and My Vassula to offer the world all that you can to attract them to receive this Heart that loves them..."**

Father O'Carroll and Vassula have lately been articulating what might be called a kind of Sacred Heart trilogy given to us from heaven over the centuries. In the revelations to St. Gertrude the Great, the inexhaustible mercy of the Divine Heart of Jesus was emphasized. Then to St. Margaret Mary Alacoque Jesus revealed that He identified Himself with His Sacred Heart and gave us that most welcome devotion to It. Now in the *True Life in God* messages to Vassula, Jesus seems to be completing this profound teaching by drawing each of us into a personal, intimate relationship with His Sacred Heart, exhorting us to invite the Sacred Heart of Jesus into every aspect of our daily lives.*

In the final message in this volume, Jesus proclaims:

> **My sons, my daughters, there is nothing equal to My Sacred Heart, for I am the Alpha and the Omega. And the ways of My Sacred Heart are delightful ways, leading into the intimacy so desired by Us** (the Holy Trinity).

Father O'Carroll tells us that although it was not until the Thirteenth-Century revelation to St. Gertrude that the Sacred Heart is first mentioned, we were indeed being prepared for the Inexhaustible Treasure even before the birth of Christ.

---

*Father Michael O'Carroll insists on stating that the idea of emphasizing the message of the Sacred Heart, and linking them in continuity with those given to St. Gertrude and St. Margaret Mary, came to him from laypeople who owe much to the writings of *True Life in God*. He hopes that readers of these messages will understand more fully reading them in the light of the Sacred Heart of Jesus.

> There were three great civilizations around the ancient Mediterranean basin: the Roman, based on law; the Greek, based on the intellect and exemplified by Aristotle and Plato, among many others; and the Jewish civilization, based on the heart and exemplified in the writings of the Old Testament wherein there are 850 references to the heart as expressing the whole person in response to the problems of life. We see this again and again in the tender, intimate language of the Psalms. Jesus, the manifestation of the divine heart, took from the Old Testament when he said, **"Blessed are the pure of heart, for they shall see God."** St. Thomas Aquinas taught that this beatitude summarizes the entire Gospel of Jesus Christ.

It was during the 1996 U.S. tour that Father O'Carroll was moved to share for the first time a personal experience he had many years ago regarding the Sacred Heart, the feast day of which was made universal in the Church only in 1856:

> I was brought up in that wonderful, inspiring world of idealism of thoughts, of insights into the life of the Savior. We were taught that He had told St. Margaret Mary of Alacoque that **"You will understand My mysteries, <u>all of them</u> through the whole of My life better now through My Heart. It is with My Heart that I shall mediate for you with the Father"...**
>
> Then after (but by no means as a result of) the Second Vatican Council, just as there was a decline in the devotion to Our Lady, devotion to the Sacred Heart of Jesus began to be dismissed as somehow out of date. I felt, as did many others, profoundly saddened by all this. I was in Cap de la Madeleine in Quebec at the great Canadian shrine of Our Lady, and one night as I was oppressed by this sadness, I saw a black spot and I was given to understand that the Lord was saying: **"It is to this that they want to reduce the vastness of My Heart,"** and then I heard a voice, **"You will live to see the revival of devotion to the Sacred Heart of Jesus."** At that time I thought I might be suffering an illusion but still I clung to the hope that this reassurance might be true. And it has turned out to be so. Jesus says in the *True Life in God* messages, **"I intend to revive devotion to My Sacred Heart."**

I have lived through the effort to suppress this devotion, but thank God, I have lived to see the reversal of it. But I would never have thought that it would come through a member of the Orthodox Church!

In November 1996, Father O'Carroll was asked in an interview for the New York television station, WPIX Channel 11 what he thought was the most important aspect of the *True Life in God* messages. Without hesitation he said that it is the way they have made the Most Blessed Trinity come alive for hundreds of thousands of souls for whom Our Heavenly Father, The Holy Spirit—and even The Second Person of the Trinity, Our Savior Jesus Christ—were only distant abstractions.

In that same month in Minneapolis, Vassula spoke on the feast day of St. Gertrude the Great and noted how Jesus had spoken to St. Gertrude and to St. Margaret Mary Alacoque about the treasures of His Sacred Heart. A recent message from Our Blessed Mother spoke of a "world that has grown cold to love," echoing the words of St. John the Evangelist when he appeared to St. Gertrude in the 13th Century. When Gertrude asked St. John why he had not spoken of this "Treasure," he answered that "to tell of the pulsations of the Heart of Jesus has been reserved for modern times, so that in hearing these things, the world already old and growing cold in the love of God, may be rekindled and grow warm again." [*Legatus Divinae Pietatis* by St. Gertrude, Book IV, Ch. IV, quoted in Volume 8 of *True Life in God*, pp. 401-402, handwriting edition]. So on St. Gertrude's feast day, November 16, Vassula read from the message given for the United States in April 1995 [excerpted here]:

As tenderly as a father treats his children, I have treated you and have revealed to your heart this Inexhaustible Treasure that had been hidden for generations and was kept for your Times. These Times when Knowledge and Faith would be despised because of the coldness of the world. My Treasure was reserved for the end of times you are now living in, when people would be preferring their own pleasure to God, rendering themselves to every evil [rather] than to good.

I am pouring out on you My Inexhaustible Treasure from My Sacred Heart.... I have for the past years, offered you all that Heaven has to offer. So tell Me, what could I have done more to save you that I have not done?

A contemplative nun has written (cf. Volume 7 of TLIG, page VIII) that the messages of *True Life in God* "...assure us that the loving heart of Jesus is planning a rescue mission far beyond our wildest dreams...." She quotes Notebook 53:47-48: "...**I had once said that from My Sacred Heart I will perform at the End of Times works as never before, works that will marvel you to show the glory of My Sacred Heart**".

Now in this ninth volume of messages, we see still more light shed on the nature of this "rescue mission"; on Jesus' vow to restore the Body of Christ on the foundations of His "primitive church"; and His promise to establish the "New Heavens and the New Earth."

The present volume opens with teachings on the Seven Gifts of the Holy Spirit. Note that Jesus had earlier emphasized "**the inner power of My Church is My Holy Spirit.**" Next come the messages on the Immaculate Heart of Mary, at which Father O'Carroll exclaimed after reading them: "There have never been more profound or more beautiful teachings given on Mary's Heart!"

For those of us who have been struck by the number of people we know personally who have been brought back to faith through what they believe to be messages from heaven, there is also in Volume 9 a particularly striking passage in the message of September 20, 1996:

> **...My Mother and I are raising disciples who become personal friends to us,...intimate, so that they will stand up like lights on a lamp-stand and shine in those days of ordeal; they will be the sturdy pillars of My Church...upheld by My Holy Spirit**

To those of us who find—often to our own astonishment and in spite of our own planning—that we are happily devoting our lives to diffusing this "Love Hymn from Heaven," it becomes clearer every day what the Lord meant when He told His Apostles: "**It is not you who have chosen Me, but I who have chosen you.**" As Father O'Carroll expressed it, "we are called now to change the neglect of His Sacred Heart into glorification." In this connection it is worth noting the remarks of Pope John Paul II in his Angelus address August 11, 1996 after which he gave his apostolic blessing to the Spanish group of spirituality of *True Life in God,* (present that day by invitation):

> I wish to all of them a fruitful summer which will help them to reaffirm their Christian promise so that their generous response to God can be the witness of His love in the world.

Father concluded a recent talk in San Francisco by quoting from a message in this volume which explains that it was because St. John the Beloved was inspired by the Sacred Heart that he was the only Apostle who stood up and was counted at Calvary:

> **You will continue to obtain from My Heart abundant sanctifying graces to accomplish your mission...I had given in the past to My beloved disciple John a glimpse of My treasures in My Heart that led him in the terrors of that day all the way to My Cross. Then later on he (John), invited Gertrude to revere My Sacred Heart, showing her the value of the treasures hidden in My Heart. Her eyes rained tears of joy when she saw those divine treasures. I've been longing to reveal to you in your day and age the riches of a mystery kept secret for endless ages. So honor My Sacred Heart and be innocent; be the salt of the earth and the light so that you will shine in the world like a bright star because you will be offering the world the Word of Life...**

Finally, this message was given in November 1996 during the 18-city tour of the U.S.:

> **...enjoy the inexhaustible riches that I had reserved for your times now and show them to the world, this world that has grown cold and is dead to love. Show My Inexhaustible Treasure to every nation and tell them that greater gift than My Sacred Heart they could not receive. And you My remnant, bless My children for Me...My Heart is touched to tears, I love you; I love you with all My Heart. ic**

Robert Carroll,
U.S. National Coordinator
True Life in God Association

Welcome

To the praise of Jesus and Mary

In reading the messages, read *Volume I* or *My Angel Daniel* first, then follow the books in order so that you become immersed in God's Love for you. You will understand while reading from the beginning that God is calling you to an intimate relationship with Him.

Jesus Christ asked me to tell you to always take my name, Vassula, out of the messages and replace it with your name. You will hear Him then speaking to you, re-animating your soul to move, aspire, and breathe in His Glory. God will draw you very delicately into His Heart so that you no longer belong to yourself but to the One who moves you in union with Their Oneness (The Holy Trinity).

I want to thank everyone who supports and helps to diffuse these messages. Jesus said on several occasions: "My message saves souls." Let everyone who is moved by the Holy Spirit become witnesses of God's Infinite Love. May you, too, become a disciple of these end-times.

Vassula

Publisher's Notes:

- Vassula uses the Jerusalem Bible for her references in the text. Occasionally there is a different chapter arrangement in the Jerusalem edition. Knowing this may help to find the references in other editions.

- In reading the messages and trying to live a "True Life in God," ask the Holy Spirit to be your spiritual director. Father Michael O'Carroll insists that he is only Vassula's "counselor" while the Holy Spirit is her "Director." He tells us, "This is the role the Holy Spirit will fulfill for each of us if we sincerely ask Him." Every difficulty encountered can be resolved most efficaciously through appeal to the Holy Spirit for direction.

Excerpts from Notebook 79

Message of 12 May 95, continued from NB 78 p.64...That I am the only true God, and Jesus Christ, My only Son

- ✠ Although you will continue to be a sign of contradiction, you will accomplish your mission with Me
- ✠ The Almighty's designs are so profound in His Messages that many will be healed
- ✠ Continue to draw every soul into the intimacy of God; attract My children into the Divine Love of God
- ✠ Every time a soul awakens and finds God, all Heaven rejoices and celebrates
- ✠ You glorify the Almighty by bringing souls to love God
- ✠ You will learn to bear your trials with astounding joy

29 May 95, NB p.9 (Galilee)...My Eyes never stopped following you from the moment you were born

30 May 95, NB p.14 (Bethlehem)...Love is the way to heaven

- ✠ Ask for the gift of love and I will give it to you
- ✠ My Love Theme is given to all nations
- ✠ Open your hearts and I will heal them
- ✠ What I see in this generation...wickedness that surpassed the wickedness of the demons
- ✠ When the sinner renounces sin to become law-abiding and honest, he deserves to live...he shall not die
- ✠ My Eyes shed tears of Blood and My Eyelids run with weeping...so very few repent
- ✠ The slightest sign of regret for your sins, and I will forgive and forget

15 June 95, NB p.19...Enter into the mystery of My Heart and receive My Peace

- ✠ Evangelize with love for Love
- ✠ Resent, My child, all that leads to evil
- ✠ I burn with a desire...to see My Church united and one
- ✠ <u>Humility and love</u>...are the keys to unity
- ✠ <u>Bow down</u> that you may see My Will; <u>lower</u> your voice so that you hear Salvation speaking to you from the heights of glory

- ✠ It is in the splendor of the Truth that you will…make everyone recognize themselves as part of one body
- ✠ I in My turn will multiply My remedies and cure you entirely…I will bring your heart in a spiritual revolution of love such as your era has never seen
- ✠ Pray for the…East and the West to join together…a pair of hands…belonging to the same body…when will those Hands of My Body lift Me over the Altar…together?
- ✠ Dedicate My treasure of My Sacred Heart to the whole earth
- ✠ I will cure many more through these messages

16 June 95, NB p. 29…Love will efface your stains and blemishes

- ✠ This is the prelude of My coming

19 June 95, NB p.33…Ask My Holy Spirit…so that you, too will not be carried away by the errors that are promulgated more and more in My Church

- ✠ Ask My Holy Spirit of Knowledge that you may not fall into the distortions being made of My Word but that you may <u>come to know Us as Thrice Holy</u>
- ✠ Ask My <u>Holy Spirit of Wisdom</u> that you look for My Heavenly Vineyard so that your soul aspires for its fruit
- ✠ Entreat and My <u>Holy Spirit of Understanding</u> will descend…with healing rays…, and all things that seemed obscure and out of your reach will be unveiled
- ✠ Do not follow a philosophy based on man's mind…come to Us instead and obtain the Gifts of the Spirit, who can transfigure your soul into Our Heaven
- ✠ Ask for My Spirit of Counsel to make you desire integrity, humility, loyalty and goodness
- ✠ I can give you My <u>Spirit of Fortitude</u>; it is not only given to My Angels but to you too; open your heart and listen
- ✠ Ask from your heart for the <u>Gift of Piety</u> and you shall obtain it;…grant me that I too may grow in love to know God and obtain His Kingdom
- ✠ Ask for the <u>Spirit of Fear</u> to discipline you into keeping My Name Holy; let My Spirit robe you with honour and reverence—a gift and a rare treasure

that I am the only true God, and Jesus Christ, My only Son, Lord of Lords, the Messiah; My teachings will give them a better knowledge of My Word, I have told you all this so that you may find peace in Me, and consolation; remember too, My daughter, that in times of danger I will lift you; I guarantee to you that you will reach the end of the road I have laid out for you; although you will continue to be a sign of contradiction, you will accomplish your

2

mission with Me, and you will glorify Me....

(Our Lady speaks)

'pethi mou',*[1] the Almighty's designs are so profound in His Message that many will be healed; My Son is with you; I am also with you; I have come to reassure you of My assistance; ... add a smiling face to all your gifts*[2]...... continue to

*[1] In Greek: 'My child'.

*[2] Our Lady in saying these words to me was smiling and had a slight tone of teasing because of my so downcast face. — Immediately while saying this to me, not only did my face brighten up, but I found myself laughing with delight.

3

please God by prophesying and showing to every nation what He has truly revealed to you so that all those who listen to you may acknowledge Him as Saviour and as Love .... continue to draw every soul into the intimacy of God; attract My children into the Divine Love of God; and you, My daughter, grow in His Spirit and never feel downcast; expand His Message as you do now and remain reassured; God-is-with-you ....

(St Michael the Archangel speaks now)

4

Vassula, have you not read: "like a young man marrying a virgin, so will the One who formed you wed you.... and as the bridegroom rejoices in his bride so does your God rejoice in you"; know this, Vassula, every time a soul awakens and finds God, all heaven rejoices and celebrates as men are happy and celebrate when they are invited to a wedding, so it is when heaven celebrates .... I wish to tell you that many times you have made Our joy in heaven increase when in your nothingness you glorify the Almighty by bringing souls

5

to love God ... so do not fear; and now write again what had been inscribed on a tablet and in a book long ago but remained to be a witness forever so that it may serve in the time to come:

" this is a rebellious people, they are lying sons, sons who will not listen to Yahweh's orders; to the seers they say, 'see no visions'; to the prophets, 'do not prophesy the truth to us; tell us flattering things; have illusory visions; turn aside from the way, leave the path, take

6

the Holy One out of our sight";* in a short time in a very short time the Holy One will come as a flame of devouring fire and surprise the haughty but the lowly will rejoice for having put their hope in Him; Salvation comes from above, Sovereignty leans down from heaven to be gracious to you; therefore, anyone who listens to His Calls and prepares himself by repenting will be like the sensible man who built his house on rock; the Lord is your Rock ♡

* Is 30 : 9-11

7

I am the guardian of your house* and the Lord the foundation of your house.... and now, daughter of the Most High, one advice: remain rooted in God, in His Love and no attack will be able to shake you; remain united in the Most Holy Trinity and you will shake your accusers by your firm resistance to temptations; remain in the Most Holy Trinity and you will have in you the strength for this battle to

* The word "house" can be understood as 'soul'. (Dn 12:1) "At that time Michael will stand up, the great prince who mounts guard over your people...."

8

hold on till the end, never giving in; you will obtain enough grace from God's own glorious power so that you accomplish your mission; everything will be done in perfect harmony and you will learn to bear your trials with astounding joy; glory to Him who is pouring on you His Graces to maintain you in His Light, His Mercy to sustain His Justice, His Strength to make you live according to His Commandments; Yahweh is just and good, full of pity for his children, faithful and true for all times, unsparingly He offers His gifts and shares His Treasures drawing each soul into His Heart; have no fear; Yahweh-is-with-you ♡

Saint Michael the Archangel of God, Yahweh;

Holy-Land - Galilee 29.5.95

(Late at night in Galilee.)

I said: "I will go to my Lord's territory and seek His Face." My heart has said of You: "Seek His Face and enjoy the sweetness of His smile, answer His Call, answer His Call to His Land."

My Lord, King! Joy of my heart; Spring of my soul, my heart exults in Your Presence and my soul rejoices in Your

10

abundant Love! My only Love come and display Your marvellous kindness in this tormented nation; Your Presence will bring them Hope; Your Eyes are known to be fixed on what is right, and Your judgement is true. Joy of my heart, are You around or are You hiding from me? are You listening at this ever so faint appeal?

My Vassula, do you know that My Eyes never stopped following you from the moment you were born? I Am all (*[1] yes!) the time with you and (*[1] yes!) present! ..... *[2] come, just a small

*[1] He asked me to underline the word three times just so as to emphasize it. Jesus was really stressing His words. *[2] A short silence.

11

prayer*; say:

blessed be Your Name,
O You who hear my prayer!
blessed are You my Lord
who removed my soul from the pit,
You have looked upon me from
the heights and humbled my soul
(from my mother's womb with fasting;) (this sentence is for me only!)

* The way Jesus said 'come, just a small prayer' was one of His typical ways of expression, after a short silence to change tone and attitude saying what followed with a rush as though we had to hurry and get going, and at the same time treating me as a weak child and He, taking a paternal attitude.

12

Blessed be Your Graciousness
who drew me in Your Heart
to save me and set me free;
God, You are my salvation,
my riches, my sight and my life,
You who daily enchant my soul
and rejoice my heart with Your
Presence,
allow Me to profit from Your Presence:
peace, integrity, love and a
spirit of forgiveness,
let every fibre of my heart

13

proclaim with love Your Glory;
hear my prayer now that I am
Your passing guest in Your country
and answer me; amen

.... this is all; let My other guests*
too, whom I bless, read this prayer;
all I ask is: love - love - love!

Jesus is My Name IC

(- I was called to witness in Ramallah, Bir Zeit, Bethlehem and Jifna.
* I was accompanied by 20 pilgrims, most of them Greek orthodox who came from the island of Rhodos, and some from Athens. Some came from France, Switzerland, Holland and Puerto Rico. The others apart from Fr. O Carroll were from Bethlehem, R. Catholics. (This message was read out in the boat on the Sea of Galilee.)

14

Back to Bethlehem 30.5.95

Vassula, I am with you and all I ask is love; tell them and let them all understand that love is the way to heaven; love conquers hearts and enlarges My Kingdom; love is the key to end up this Apostasy; love is given to you freely, ask for the gift of love and I will give it to you! My Love Theme* is given to all nations and those who want to hear it will hear it; ♡ pray, pray, pray but do it with

* This message

love; open your hearts and I will heal them; repay evil with love, seek good and Goodness from above will answer you and turn you into Our likeness. I know all things and I observe all things and what I see in this generation is not according to Our likeness; insolence, violence, greed, vainglory, wickedness that surpassed the wickedness of the demons, rebellion against Me and all that is holy, and all the vices that can bring your soul to ruin are what most of this

16

generation practises; every kind of wrong-doing is sin.... lift your eyes and be eager to find Me and do not fall victims to worldly beauty, for the worship of that sort of beauty is the cause of so much evil, to crown now your wickedness you embroidered your plan to the likeness of the beast and together*, generation, you will commit your crime:

to abolish My Perpetual Sacrifice and erect in its place the disastrous abomination.

* With the beast

17

have you not heard: "when the upright man renounces his integrity to commit sin and dies because of this, he dies because of the evil that he himself has committed, but when the sinner renounces sin to become law-abiding and honest, he deserves to live; he has chosen to renounce all his previous sins; he shall certainly live; he shall not die;"* My Eyes shed tears of Blood and My Eyelids run with weeping, O what sorrow you cause Me, generation!

* Ez: 18: 26-28

18

because Death has climbed into your house and you do not realize it! so very few repent .... but most of you, generation, are not saying what you ought to: you do not repent of your wickedness saying: 'what have I done with my life, my soul and my heart?' the slightest sign of regret for your sins, and I will forgive and forget; happy the ones who meditate on My words and My appeal and reason with good sense, they shall be saved; I bless you with all My Heart I bless

19

you ♡ ic

15. 6. 95

Your Word, my King, is a healing balm; when my life was more ignoble than clay, Your Word was uttered in my ear and the invisible swiftly became visible and like a world unknown to me, like a light unknown to the blind, everything suddenly was shining with brilliant light. Like brightly blazing stars that illuminate the heavens by night, Your Word gave me sight to enter into Your Mystery. I bless You, my Lord, for Your Love now is visible before my eyes bringing my soul to live in loyalty to You for ever and ever.

yes! enter into the mystery of My Heart and receive My Peace; flower, never substitute your time of writing with other things; you have all day and I will be pleased if you come to Me in meditation; remember: love is always patient, so be patient too; do not run ahead of Me as you have done in these past days... love, true love, will endure trials, set-backs and the lot; have Me as first and above all; evangelize with love for Love and glorify Me; resent, My child, all that leads to evil and immerse yourself into all that is good and holy and which will lead you into eternal life; I am Holy and Good....* — I burn with a desire....

Which desire, my Lord?

to see My Church united and one.....
pray for unity and do not listen to those who do not want unity; the Divider keeps them separated and aggressive in their spirit; — anyone who does not work sincerely and with all his heart for unity is seriously grieving My Holy Spirit

* Suddenly our Lord stopped, and with another tone of voice, like someone who wants to confide his secret said what followed.

I implore those who assemble to lead My Church into one to impress on their minds those words:

- humility and love -

humility and love are the keys to unity; it is not the eloquence of speech nor the lengthy discourse that will lead them to unity; it is not their exchange of praise on one another that will lead My Church into one; all these things weary Me .... devastation and ruin have penetrated into My Sanctuary, so what praise can they exchange on one another? where is their honour? bow down that you may see My Will; lower your voice so that you hear Salvation speaking to you from the heights of glory; it is in your conversion that your heart will hear Me and lead My Church into one, unifying My Body; it is in the splendour of the Truth that you will fragrance again and will make everyone recognize himself as part of one body; it is in the sharing that you will

24

lead everyone close to one another; for this you need to change in your heart and flower with conversion; if you do these things and wash your heart clean of your sin, I, in My turn, will multiply My remedies and will cure you entirely; I will bring upon you a spiritual growth which will bring the remnant of My creation to abide under your roof; if you, you who ceased to be, allow My Holy Spirit, the Giver of Life, to entice you, I will bring your heart in a

25

spiritual revolution of love such as your era has never seen .... ah .... daughter, pray for the house of the East and the West to join together, like two hands when joined in prayer, a pair of hands, similar, and in beauty when joined together pointing towards heaven when in prayer; let those two Hands, belonging to the same body work together and share their capacity and resources with each other .... let those two Hands lift Me together, ah .... when will those

Hands of My Body lift Me over the Altar, holding Me together*? O come! I do not want lengthy discourses, anyone who wants to be first and best among you must be slave to all; I am here! look to yourself! and there are endless treasures in My Heart; so do not say: "where, where can I find my answers?" equip yourself with this treasure of My Heart and you will bring together

* Christ means over Mass, during the Eucharistic prayer.

27

those that have been led astray and I will reign over them all and you will dedicate My treasure of My Sacred Heart to the whole earth; — and you, daughter: by giving Me your time you please Me and it honours Me; loving Me rejoices Me and glorifies Me; desiring Me infatuates Me; the amount given to Me from your heart is the amount you will be given back from My Throne; My grace is upon you and My Hand on yours .... rest in Me; I love you and the Father loves you for loving Me;

I love You Love ....

I will cure many more through these messages; do your part, My Vassula, and I will complete your work in My Divinity; come, I will be with you while you do your other small duties*; I, Jesus, love you, have My blessings

AΩ

* *Housework of course ....*

16.6.95

In the sin of my soul You visited me with love. You have not come with stick to reprimand me, nor has Your Splendour come to me with grudge, You have, instead, visited my soul with blessings to heal its darkness.

Lover of Your creation, help us all and teach us what is pleasing to You, so that everything we do will be acceptable in Your Eyes.

As You know, Lord, sin has become the oracle of the wicked, we sin as much as we breathe. Why this violent uproar among Your creation? Why this impurity? Why this revolt?

I bow down in reverence of You and ask You:

For how long will Your sons and daughters continue to be put to confusion

30

by the Evil one? In Your saving justice, my Lord, help us, and tell us what is needed most to change.

peace be with you; I am delighted to hear you; all I need is love, love, love; love can do everything; so love Me and continue to grow in My Love, then no obscure spot would remain in you; Love will efface your stains and blemishes; Love heals, it amends; Love brings good fruit, fruit that lasts .... have you not heard, My child, that everyone who loves is one

31

of My Own and knows Me? have you not heard that on Judgement Day you will be judged according to the measure of your love? you asked Me and said: "why this violent uproar among Your creation? why this impurity? why this revolt?" My dear child, this is the prelude of My coming; you, who love Me, will have to suffer only for a little while, you who bow down before My power will be recompensed; you who have not forgotten your Maker will see

32

Me in My Glory .... My Return is as certain as the dawn ; you ask, daughter: " tell us what is needed most to change, " I need faithful love, for faithful love is what pleases Me;

Consoler of Your kin, Friend of mankind, Light thrice Holy, Beloved of the Father, Starlight of the night, Mountain of Incense and Myrrh, Delight of the Father, Infatuation of Your Mother, draw us all in Your love, ravish our heart with one single glance, call us into Your Kingdom since You delight in showing faithful love, convert us in Your Flame of Love.

Let this terror of the night before us come to its end and we shall all contemplate Your saving justice.

I just wanted to hear this from you again; flower, I will continue using you; My well-beloved come now and enjoy resting in My Heart; I, Jesus, who raised you, love you and bless you;

19. 6. 95

peace be with you .... dress My Wounds with love in My Holy Spirit; seek always My Holy Spirit; come and learn:

to preserve your soul from any ill-dispositions and from temptations, ask My

34

Holy Spirit, the Giver of Life, to govern you in holiness and help you grow in grace and wisdom so that you, too, will not be carried away by the errors that are promulgated more and more in My Church; ask My Holy Spirit of Knowledge that you may not fall into the distortions being made of My Word but that you may come to know Us* as thrice Holy, and by knowing Us know yourself in Our Reflection, in Our Image;

* The Most Holy Trinity

35

I am saying, 'you too', because many of whom I have raised have either slackened or have fallen .... they deserted My holy rules with which I had entrusted them; they failed Me because they gave in to their impulses .... they did not place Me as first*, they have placed __their__ interests first, not Mine; ask My __Holy Spirit of Wisdom__ that you look for My Heavenly Vineyard so that your soul aspires for its fruit; come and entreat My Holy Spirit of Wisdom to visit you

* I also understood: they did not place love as first.

36

in your poverty; in your poverty He will not flee; He will befriend you and court you and in His pure emanation will make your spirit revolve only around heavenly things, asking Us* for what is holy and imperishable; My Holy Spirit of Wisdom will show you Our* Kingdom, a Kingdom of piety reserved for the upright and holy; so do not be like those who break My Heart daily and grieve My Spirit without ceasing by becoming a constant rebel, a Cain without

* Holy Trinity

37

mercy; set your heart right and My Spirit of Wisdom will be your guide and director to lead you into Our Kingdom which has been prepared for you since the foundation of the world; entreat and My Holy Spirit of Understanding will descend in your nothingness as a brilliant sun with healing rays in your eyes, and all things that seemed obscure and out of your reach will be unveiled, and in your nothingness My Spirit of Understanding will lead you into the mystery of the Divine Truth ♡

38

do not let My Spirit find you ill-disposed or unwilling, let Him enlighten your mind and in the contrast of your nothingness My Holy Spirit of Understanding will be Everything you lack; Companion and Friend. He will hide no mysteries from you, but will offer you teachings that no mind has understood, things beyond the mind of mankind, going into the impenetrable and into the imperishable, reaching the depths of God; so do not be like the scholars and the philosophers of your

39

time who justify their philosophy to the model of their own rationalistic spirit; flesh and blood cannot reveal what comes from the Spirit; I can offer you My Kingdom and My Spirit can lead your step into My Kingdom ♡ come then and inherit what lasts for ever by allowing My Spirit of Understanding to enlighten your mind and your body with His Divine Light, allowing Him to animate your soul in the intimacy We* desire of

* The plural form represents the Holy Trinity.

40

you in Us; My sons, My daughters, come to Us in your silence to obtain the gifts We can offer you ♡ thrice holy is Our Name; do not follow a philosophy based on man's mind, for the viper will nest in you; come to Us instead and obtain the Gifts of the Spirit, who can transfigure your soul into Our Heaven; ask Us from your heart and you shall obtain; acknowledge Us in Our Trinitarian Holiness and you shall be called "Our child, Our Own"; for We shall make out of your soul a living portrait of Our Holiness, a visible image of the Invisible, an attraction to all the sacred things that have been declared to you for your salvation from the beginning of Time listen and understand: you want to be kin to the Holy Spirit of Counsel and make sure you will gain heaven? acknowledge Us in Our Trinitarian Holiness and you will be lifted by Our angels to discover Him-who-is ask for counsel and you will be counselled to do good all the days of your life; the Kingdom is prepared for you who do good; learn to repay evil with love; you know the Commandments and you also know that on the two greatest hang all the Law and the prophets; you do not have to be rich to enter into My Kingdom nor learned; My Kingdom is given to the poor in spirit and to those who call out: "God, be merciful to me, a sinner;" My Kingdom is given to mere children and to the lowly who know how to call out: "Abba!" seek Me, your Lord, I am Love; seek Love all you, the humble of the earth, who obey My Commandments; ask for My Spirit of Counsel to make you desire integrity, humility, loyalty and goodness so that your step will not fail you and do wrong; unfailingly My Spirit of Counsel will make His Law known to you and counsel you saying: "do not equal anyone to God; serve the cause of right; lift the oppressed; do no harm to anyone, but love and help one another; do not afflict or harass the widow or show harshness to the orphan; practise goodness and do not be like the villains and the wicked who ruin their souls by ruining the helpless; never rebel against your God but bow your head and bend your knee in His Holy Presence; never substitute His Perpetual Sacrifice, not even for all the kingdoms of the world and their splendour; be alert to those counsels and you shall fragrance and your happiness will be like a river, breaking into several rivulets announcing and counselling others to seek the Kingdom of Heaven and the glory of Our Trinitarian Holiness which can adorn your spirit in Our Splendour for ever and ever ♡ – have I not strength to save? with one word I bless and save; so do not lie helpless; I can give you My Spirit of Fortitude; it is not only given to My angels but to you too; open your heart and listen, ask and it shall be given to you; I can make you

46

preach My Word and My Tradition thrice blessed, to the utmost of your capacity by the power of My Spirit of Fortitude; happy are you who will obtain My Gift* and through this Gift obtain strength to live in obedience of faith, in righteousness, joy and peace; so do not lie helpless and with fear; I tell you, do not fear the taunts of men nor be dismayed by their insults, for the moth shall eat them like garments, since from the

* Holy Spirit of Fortitude

beginning they have been in communion with the evil one. I will be your Strength and you shall no longer walk alone; I and you, you and I will bear, together, the crosses given to you for your sanctification; My Spirit of Fortitude can clothe you in My Strength to bear witness to the Truth, the Alpha and the Omega, with zeal and courage. My Holy Spirit of Fortitude can help you overcome all the obstacles that come in your way that prevent you from reaching Me; in

48

the power of My Spirit you will become like a warrior filled with courage and strength; fortified by His power you will fortify My Sanctuary against the enemy and against transgression; like the sun you will shine in Our Presence thrice Holy; like a fire your words will flare like a torch; like a sword that cuts and pierces your prophecies will strike, dragging the kingdoms of the world down to destruction; in the power of My Spirit you will obtain the inaccessible, you will attain the unattainable; every one of your achievements will show Our magnificence in Our Trinitarian Glory, so do not say: "where, where shall we find sufficient power and fortitude to glorify God?" My marvels lie in the Spirit, Invisible, yet visible through His powerful action, Inaccessible to the touch yet all around you and within you; who can attempt to understand the way My Spirit moves? ask My Holy Spirit of Fortitude to grant you His radiant

50

Strength for My Interests and I, I will pass on to you without reserve sufficient power to join in the battle of your times with Michael the Archangel, and combat evil and blasphemy, distortion of My Word and rebellion against all that is holy; deign and ask Me to grant you the Spirit of Fortitude to enable you to reach out your hand to the cup I will offer you; these are the things you should ask before My Saints and Our Trinitarian Holiness; then you, too, will practise endurance in the battle of the Great Day* to be the defender of the Truth, and bring all people to acknowledge Us as thrice Holy but One, in the unity of essence ♡ and We will invite each one of them to enter into the mystery of the True Knowledge of Our Trinitarian Holiness by dressing them in grace and beauty and ceremonial vestments, Our richest clothes:

- Divinity which emanates

* Ap. 16:14

52

from Us, leading them into Eternal Life;

- <u>Light</u> thrice Holy, glittering in their soul and body to live in Us for ever and ever;

- <u>Truth</u> and <u>Love</u>, to know the True God thrice Holy;

- <u>Faith</u>, victory over all the world, harvest of Eternal Life;

come, come you who say: "I cannot obtain redemption for I have not received the piety to enter into God's Kingdom;" ask from your heart for the <u>Gift of</u>

53

Piety and you shall obtain it; say:
'Holy Spirit, Giver of Life,
Holy Spirit, Thrice Holy,
grant me that I, too, may
grow in love to know God
and obtain His Kingdom;
grant me the Spirit of Piety
so that my spirit grows in
the principles of the Saints
and that my thoughts turn
into Your Thoughts,
my acts into Your Acts which

54

are all pure and divine;
Holy Spirit of Piety,
Friend of God
teach me to reach perfection
and control over every part
of myself which is so evil,
so that I may obtain Eternal Life;
Spirit of Piety
ever so beautifully dressed,
come to me and dress my spirit
in purity that I, too, may be
pleasing in God's Eyes;

55

dress my soul with a living Spirit
to serve the Holy Trinity
with honour and grace;
let me die to my principles,
let me die to my partiality,
my tepidity, my lethargy
and my ambitions;
come and revive me into Your Purity;
Supplier of the fruit of
the Tree of Life,
Eternal Joy,
grant me Your Spirit too

56

to be kin to the Holy Trinity
and an heir* to Your Kingdom;
let my tongue taste what is
most pure in the Light of God
thrice Holy
and consume the One who said:
"I am the Bread of Life;"
Holy Spirit of Life,
thrice Holy,
grant my spirit to attain
perfection in the Science

* Could be heiress too.

of the Spirit of Piety;
to learn how to observe with fear
what is real Flesh and real Food,
what is real Blood and real Drink
so that I may live in the
Father, in the Son and in the
Holy Spirit,
Trinitarian but One, in the
unity of essence;
make my soul work for Your intentions
which are holy and redemptive,
most pleasing in Your Eyes;

58

by entering my soul
Your Spirit of Piety
will turn me into a devout and
fervent servant;
Starlight of my soul,
pass on to me the piety
of your Saints
to keep Your Laws holy and
graciously show Yourself to my wretched
soul to remind me that
incorruptibility will bring me near
the Trinitarian God

59

Most Powerful and Most Holy,
hence nothing impure will be able
to find its way in me ♡ Amen' ic
the Spirit of Piety will lead you to become:
- a delight of the Delight of the Father,
- a fragrance of myrrh in My Presence,
- a lily of My garden; - a boast* to My
angels; - a festival of joy permanently in
My Heart, and a copy of Myself; - you
will only have to will and I will lift your
pitiable soul! I do not lack means to
show My Power or My Sovereignty;

* In the sense of being glorified.

60

come and seek Me in simplicity of the heart, do not remain in debt to your sin, ask for forgiveness and I shall forgive you; ask for the Spirit of Fear to discipline you into keeping My Name Holy; let My Spirit robe you with honour and reverence - a gift and a rare treasure, a sign of loving faithfulness - learn to bow your head low so that I may be seen, learn to lower your voice so that you may begin to hear My Voice and discover My intentions, My desires and My Will,

61

learn to raise your voice only in praise for My Glorious Presence; learn to raise your head only in search of Me and of what is heavenly.... many influential men have been put low, for they have neither honoured Me nor shown Me any reverence; you want to know what 'the Fear of the Lord' means? the Fear of the Lord is the beginning of Wisdom, the Fear of the Lord is the crown of Wisdom ♡ it is he who receives Me graciously, acknowledging Us as Thrice Holy with reverence, faithfulness and honour; to Fear Me is to humble yourself in Our Presence, pleading with Me to forgive you so that I make out of you an everlasting altar on which I would place all My Knowledge, My Precepts and My Law; I will place on your Holy Fear My confidence, My treasures, with learned sayings revealing My mysteries and My secrets; I will show you the mysteries of My Heart, those hidden treasures in your Holy Fear and you will learn then that I am God in whom you can

63

obtain Everlasting Life, Everlasting Joy and Peace; you will learn from My Spirit of Fear that submissiveness seduces Me; stern as it might appear, it is The Opening for Me to enter in your heart and do My Will; I will receive your submission with your Holy Fear as one receives a royal crown of splendour and We, the Trinitarian God, for Our part, will dress you in Our invincible Holiness so that any trace of lawlessness remaining in you will dissipate from you like morning mist;

born and renewed by My Spirit, you who, in My grief had ceased to be, will once more be ♡ many of the dead will look at you, uncomprehending, that you, once dead but now alive behave as We would have you behave, sagaciously and with Holy Fear; learn that the Lord of All offers grace and mercy for those who fear Him ♡ and fear His Name; I will get My honour, if you praise My Name thrice Holy, everywhere you go; and that incense* offered to Me from your heart

* It means: prayers

Excerpts from Notebook 80

19 June 95, continued from NB #79, p.64...Lower yourself so that in My Mercy My arms lift you

- ✠ Since your intentions, generation, are to to trample on My Perpetual Sacrifice…I shall do to you what I have done to Sodom and Gomorrah but one hundred times more
- ✠ Lift your eyes to Heaven and you will see My angels weeping
- ✠ You are displeased with the one who sits on Peter's Chair and who reminds you constantly to keep My rules holy
- ✠ My Church will unite in the end…and My Prayer to the Father will be fulfilled
- ✠ My Father will strip you of everything you own setting aflame your ten Towers and laying their foundations bare; all your precious stones will be shattered
- ✠ Every effort, every step forward done for unity is blessed thrice from the Father, Myself and the Holy Spirit

4 July 95, NB p.13 (Curitiba—Brazil)...If you have tasted My Goodness you will act with goodness too towards others

7 July 95, NB p.14 (Joinville—Brazil) Beware of conflicts that arise in your midst to disturb the harmony I have given you...My work is done in peace, harmony and joy

- ✠ I need sacrifices to bring the Two Sisters together!

9 July 95, NB p.17 (Sao Carlo—Brazil)...Allow Me to show My Portrait to this generation by using your hand; I want My children to know Me more

31 July 95, NB p.18...You will get My answer to your request,—regarding Japan

- ✠ You all have a place in My Heart since you are all sharing and defending My Work
- ✠ My Holy Spirit had explicitly named this Work: "True Life in God"

1 August 95, NB p.23...Daughter all I have is yours

✠ I only ask for your friendship...and a word to Me showing Me that you have not forgotten Me

✠ My lamb, the world hated Me as it hates you now

16 August 95, NB p.26...I come to meet you with blessings

✠ Human strength shall never prevail in My Plan of salvation

✠ Build and plant in My service and I, I shall knock down and overthrow your aggressors

6 September 95, NB p.30...I own you, and you, My daughter, and you own Me

✠ Allow yourself to be repressed as My Own Son, your Redeemer, was repressed

27 September 95, NB p.43...never mind what is beyond your means and your strength for I will fill up what lacks

✠ I intend to continue keeping My veil on your eyes so that you will have no opportunity...becoming elated

29 September 95 (St Michael's feastday), NB p.48...Do you know what is holding back the wrath of God Almighty?

✠ Never cease asking Me for my intercession

2 October 95 (Feast of our guardian angels), NB p.52...I will always guard you, forever I shall guide you

6 October 95, NB p.57...I will be your sole Guide, when you lie down, your faithful Watchman, when you wake, your cheerful Companion

✠ I am reduced to beg for your generosity

✠ I would go back to Calvary...to save you from your Apostasy

✠ I need generosity and warmth, a proof of love...I do not regret coming to you

in My Name is like a pure offering to Me; it is time to seek for this gift of My Spirit of Fear, - weapon for combating rebellion - element to prevent you from falling and sceptre of My Kingdom - stoop down to Me and I will lift you lovingly; lower yourself so that in My Mercy My arms lift you, like someone who lifts an infant close against his cheek will I lift you, caress you and love you and I will never part with you ♡

in these days and in your times I am

2

confronted by the guilt of those who strike Me and the wickedness of those who practise deceit, "do not commit this abomination which the prophet Daniel spoke of," I say, but your steps persistently follow Deceit; your era is challenging My Power; very well then, since your intentions, generation, are to trample on My Perpetual Sacrifice and abolish It, I tell you: I shall do to you what I have done to Sodom and Gomorrah but one hundred times more, to equal your sins; – you see those ten Towers you have built for yourselves as Lodges? well, you will <u>never</u> live in them, your empire will crumble down together with you, and those precious stones you have treasured? you will never possess them, for I am going to pass through you to remind you that from the Beginning My Name, <u>thrice Holy,</u> was to be honoured and kept Holy and that your due to Me was to fear Me;

— come, you who still err in this wilderness, undecided and weak! come and ask for these seven gifts of My Holy Spirit

4

and I, the Author of heaven and earth, Word and God, will lavish you with My gifts; I will offer you, to save you, My seven gifts; to prosper you into a delightful vineyard I will teach you temperance and prudence, justice and fortitude; come to Me, I who am thrice Holy; come, and with the power of My Breath I will turn you into an untarnished mirror to reflect on you and in you: Our Divinity, and you will live in Us thrice Holy, for ever and ever;

5

soul!* exposed now to the injustice of the world, obtain Our Peace and Love; with you I Am; are you still willing to work for peace, unity and love?

I am willing to work for peace, unity and love, yes!

be observant then of My rules.... be patient and remember, remember what I had endured; be content with what I have already given you and do not seek for more; continue to be conscientious in your work ♡

* God turned suddenly to me and addressed me.

6

in the beginning of My Message I said: "dress My Wounds with your love," I am wounded beyond recognition; lift your eyes to heaven and you will see My angels weeping.... ah, generation, you are fanning My Father's wrath, you are fanning His wrath which will light up and burst into flames and when it does, He will come to you as a devouring flame of fire and burn you into ashes together with your iniquity and your rebellion with all the evil disguised today as good; alas for

7

you, you who are disguised as servants of righteousness* serving in My Church but are none other than counterfeit servants, serving the rules of the Beast, I tell you: unless you repent, you will draw upon you My Father's wrath and end up in flames too; you are displeased with the one who sits on Peter's Chair and who reminds you constantly to keep My rules holy, since they are sacred; you are displeased at his calls of ecclesia's

* The Cains of today - the apostates who spread errors - those who want to abolish the Perpetual Sacrifice - those who contradict the Pope for wanting to keep the Tradition of the Church as in the Primitive Church - and those who combat Unity.

8

Tradition and of living daily a Eucharistic life; you are anguished when it comes to approaching the Eastern Church with the Western Church and perform Unity! faithless and perverted generation! how much longer must I put up with your rebellion?
but I tell you: whatever you fear will come true; whatever you dread will be realized; My Church will unite in the end and will be One and My Prayer to the Father will be fulfilled; will you now still persist in your evil designs? one day, servants of the

Beast, together with the False Prophet, alias the second Beast, you will bear the weight of your faults, and they will be as grave as Death; today still, in secrecy, you* are aiming at Peter's Chair, using your people whom you placed on high seats to masquerade the Truth with liberalism and the lot; you are plundering My sacred Law and devouring it, to eliminate My Tradition; this is why My Father will strip you of everything you own, setting aflame your ten Towers and laying

* The Beast and his followers

10

their foundation bare; all your precious stones will be shattered and yourself consumed by fire; unless I hear from you your cry of repentance I will execute all these things in a very short time, ecclesia will revive!
— flower, I am with you and before you I stand and bless you; every effort, every step forward, done for unity is blessed thrice from the Father, Myself and the Holy Spirit; let this be known and tell everyone to work and pray for unity; and if anyone comes to you and asks

II

what would please Me most, say to them:
" the feast of the kingdom of God is at hand, therefore, be ready to address your prayers to God for the salvation of strayed souls; gather together and pray that ecclesia will be one; pray with conviction and God will hear you; there is no one who has prayed, sacrificed and fasted for the sake of the kingdom of God who has not been heard or given repayment a hundred times over in his present time and in the world to come;

12

also that he has not inherited Eternal Life;" give them that word and ask them to remember My words in Scriptures: (Mt 12: 34-37) 'a man's words flow out of what fills his heart; a good man draws good things from his store of goodness; a bad man draws bad things from his store of badness; so I tell you this, that for every unfounded word men utter they will answer on Judgement day, since it is by your words you will be acquitted, and by your words condemned'; — display My Holiness and

be eager to serve Me as now; I love you,
I, your Master but Friend as well and
your Beloved of your heart! have My Peace
and blessings — this is all for now, I
Am is with you, come, we, us? Jesus is
My Name, keep it holy; ΙΧΘΥΣ 

Curitiba - Brazil - 4.7.95

daughter, peace be with you, remember, all
I really need is love; tell them* to learn to
love Me, to learn to adore Me; did you
not know that at the end everyone will be

* In my conference and testimony

14

judged according to the measure of his love? if you have tasted My Goodness you will act with goodness too towards others; open your heart and invite Me so that you get to know Me; Love is by your side ♡

Joinville, Brazil 7.7.95

My Vassula, I, Jesus give you My Peace, this Peace that no one should take away from you! beware of conflicts that arise in your midst to disturb the harmony I have given you and the flow of peace My Work gives to you, listen now and take this as

15

My advice: work as you have always worked with Me; My Work is done in peace, harmony and joy; I delight when I find your heart well-disposed and eager to please Me; walk with Me and allow My Heart to talk to you; when I speak, write My Words as you have done, and as you write, I bless you and all of what you write; love Me and I am praised in your love and honoured;

love Me and console Me;

love Me and you will never perish;

16

love Me and I will unite My Church in your love,

love Me and for the sake of your love, My Father's wrath can be diminished;

love Me and join in the saints' prayers; — all I ask from all of you is love; all I need from all of you is your heart; I need your hearts to build unity *in* your hearts; Vassula, I *need* *sacrifices* to bring the Two Sisters* together!

* The Lord speaks about the R. Catholic Church and the Orthodox Church as Two Sisters.

17

– flower, I tell you that My honour and praise, I have received during your mission in Brazil; ic

São Carlo - Brazil - 9. 7. 95

Yahweh is My Name, daughter, listen to My Voice: I am your Keeper who delights in you, allow Us* to imbue you with Our Knowledge so that We instruct all of you; allow Me to show My Portrait to this generation by using your hand; I want My children to know Me more; glorify

* The Holy Trinity

your Father in Heaven; I, Yahweh, love you ♡ AΩ

31. 7. 95

I Am is with you, so allow Me now to use with you My gift that will honour My Name; for, My child, through this gift I brought many back to Me; so peace be with you! yes! you will get My answer to your request, – regarding Japan*: you have all shared

* The Association of Japan of True Life in God.

19

together, in My graces to you all, the power of healing through My given Messages; I it is who establish the associations of True Life in God; I offer prayers to the Father for your partnership in the Messages I am giving; you all have a place in My Heart since you are all sharing and defending My Work; Satan, in his jealousy, wishes to sift you all like wheat: to fail; so stand your ground with prayer as your weapon; be sympathetic and generous to one another, be

20

patient with one another as I am patient with you; be tolerant with one another as the Father is tolerant with this generation; forgive each other as readily as I forgive when forgiveness is asked !! I had warned you that working for Me, hardships are certain to come, and that is what each one of you has found out; but do not despair, I am with you so long as you remain faithful to Me, so rely on Me, I will continue to give you strength, courage and hope;

21

now hear Me and understand: My Holy Spirit had explicitly named this Work: "True Life in God", but some of you listened to deceitful spirits and gave way to them .... take care of all the Divine Work that has been entrusted to you and turn away from disputes that will lead you to division; can you not see? can you not discern how the Evil One is at work? you ought to turn your minds more attentively than before to what the Spirit offered so that you do not drift away from My Grace; with this in view, do your best to work with harmony and peace, gentleness and understanding; My dear friends, remember: do not wreck the Holy Spirit's Work by allowing yourselves to give rise to harmful talk; I tell you: rejoice in the Spirit and seek His Ways in which He will keep you devout, united and happy in the reflection of His Love; IXΘYΣ 

23

1. 8. 95

My Lord and my God, show me the light of Your Divine Face; Maker in glory, Your arrows on me do not make me run away from You; on the contrary, I am here, quivering with impatience to listen to You; come and satisfy my hunger!

daughter, all I have is yours; I love you; never doubt of My Love; love Me and you shall live; live holy and pray more; the devil never wearies of attacking you and from tempting you; so stay vigilant and never weary of writing; never abandon your prayers, never cease being with Me*; I am always with you,

* In prayer, we are together with the Lord.

24

and I never leave you, but, daughter, I want also this from you; in these days* where you and your family are together I do not ask a great deal from you nor do I call you to obtain lengthy messages, I only ask for your friendship, your love, your attention from time to time and a word to Me showing Me that you have not forgotten Me; see? Vassula, do not worry about your

* My family and I were passing our holidays together.

25

oppressors; do not worry on things that
belong to the world, all these will
wear out but My Love for you will
remain forever and for all eternity;
My lamb, the world hated Me as it
hates you now, but it is only the
world and this world <u>will</u> wear
away! come, remain near Me and My
Mother who loves you! have Our Peace ♡
we, us?

ΙΧΘΥΣ 

26

16. 8. 95

Lord, my Yahweh, never let the world drag my steps back into its entrails; never let it become my master nor my domain. May you grant me, my Father, what You carry most preciously in Your Heart, so let Your desires become my flesh and bones, my being, my nourishment and my life.
I love you to madness, my Strength, my Holy One thrice Holy, my Drink of Everlasting Source of Divinity and Life, my Kindness and my Tenderness, come! come to me and I promise You, Heavenly Father, to sing Your Hymn of Love to all nations to honour Your Fatherly Love.
Will my Good Lord respond from His Holy heavens? will He give His response to this sinner, to this unworthy clay?

I, Yahweh bless you; I will refresh your soul, My Name is engraved now on your heart listen: I come to meet you with blessings; daughter, you have asked for life, My delightful child, I am Life and I am here with you now; I will never abandon you; ah Vassula, let Me reassure you: human strength shall never prevail in My Plan of Salvation; I am <u>the</u> Author of this book; although your enemies avoid the light lest they be revealed, but wait for you in darkness to pounce on you; do not be afraid, My Eyes are watching

28

over you; no earthborn human will strike My child; yes, you will be calumniated and abused, but have you not seen the result of My good Works? I am telling you this to encourage you; although the Beast and its followers will keep on hounding you as hunters after their game, do not be afraid, they will not reach their aim; as I once said: they will try and erase you altogether from the surface of the earth; they will redouble in strength but not one of them

29

will be able to touch My territory and My property; — you are My Territory and My Property — I have you encircled by many angels who guard you, and I, Myself, am your Sentinel; for your own part, build and plant in My service and I, I shall knock down and overthrow your aggressors who in reality are My aggressors; as for your persecutors, pray for them; show kindness and mercy, repay evil with love; My Presence is all around you and wherever you are ♡

A Ω

6. 9. 95

Like a strayed sheep I had gone my way; from arid ground I had tried to nourish my soul and from the dry rock I had hoped to receive my drink.

Ah, my injuries from lacking were devouring me, and my sins appeared to be incurable. The mere sight of me was a scandal to Your angels, an abomination to Your Eyes, O Most Holy Trinity, most pure God. Your angels and saints stood aghast and stupefied at my total rebellion.

Day in, day out, I went about, Lacking. I trod in the shadows of the night parched with thirst, spent the night

31

fatherless, huddling instead thistles and thorns. Starved out of my flesh I could not comprehend why had this misery befallen me? Why had the light of my eyes left me?

O evil inclination, did you expect sympathy? My downfall was greeted with an immense applause by a multitude of demons for they had managed to pluck me from my Shepherd's Fold, and rob me from my Sight, my Joy, my Love and my Life.... and when life in me was just about to trickle away forever, You, Father! You came with stupendous power and glory. And with immense pity, You, Father, tore the heavens to reach me, from Your holy dwelling, You descended dressed in fearful splendour.

There, You were standing majestically in front of a bewildered Wretch.

32

He who prevades and permeates all things was now in the company of Wretchedness. Reeling as though with wine, my soul staggered in the Presence of this Pure Emanation Thrice Holy ....

I stuttered to pronounce, to utter something, but no sound was ever heard. I Lacked. The Fingers then that formed me suddenly reached out and were posed on my lips, opening them for me to draw in the air of His Breath. And as I inhaled a scent like choice myrrh, a wail came out of me just as a new-born, and I was instantly restored.

" From now on Your Creator will be Your Husband, My Name: Yahweh Sabaoth " (Is 54:5) He said.

" I have taken pity on you .... did you not Know, My child,

33

that I am rich in forgiving? Depart not and do not fear. Remain with Me and I will lift you and bring you home to heal you entirely.

My great Love challenged My Mercy and My Heart was touched by your misery.

Come, and if you wish I will make you a witness of My great Love I have for all of you."

— This is what Your Holy Lips uttered, every one of Your Words falling on my parched soul, like morning dew, — and while still talking, my soul, struck with remorse, found itself succumbing in its Father's Arms, in its Father's Grace

I then turned to the Lord and entreated Him to possess Him, with all my heart I said: "I want to possess

34

You, my God and Creator, as much as You possess me." Then You put around me bonds that linked me to You, bonds that would remain forever.

and I said: I shall grant you the favour of My Heart and Soul for I am Divine and Thrice Holy; I am your Father and I own you, and you, My daughter, and you own Me; did you not know that I am Grace and Mercy? come, do not ask: "why has all this happened to me?" your great misery pulled Me down from heaven; your

35

disconsolate soul made My Heart cry out to My angels and saints: "how much longer should I see her go on like this?" and to you: "Paraskevi, raise your eyes now and look at Me; I promise you that Hope will not be given to you alone, but to all, all those who are thirsty; has anyone heard anything like this? and as for you, Paraskevi, I will take you into My service and make out of you a Tree; your roots will be growing in My Garden so that your foliage remains

36

green, so that your fruit has My Name inscribed on it; and I, Myself, will be your Keeper and water you from My Fountain of Living Water .... and, as Companion and Friend, I will give you Wisdom who will educate and raise you to transmit, later on, this Hope in perfection to all mankind ♡ you will be reared by Me and formed in My Courts; this is why you will be contradicted in your journey; the world will spit on you, but not

37

more than they spat on My Son; traitors will come your way, but none of them greater than Judas; denials and rejections, too, will follow, yet none of them more severe than the rejections and denials that My Son received; pitilessly you will be misunderstood by many, but rejoice! do not fall into distress, make no resistance and do not turn away either; allow yourself to be repressed as My Own Son, your Redeemer, was repressed, scandalizing all His

38

disciples; I command you to remain untouched by the insults of men and not to respond, as My Son did not respond but remained silent ♡ and in these sufferings I will establish Peace; in your torments I will console the disconsolate; I will make your oppressors oppress you and while you will be lying down in torments, trampled underfoot by men, I will be setting light in the Church, giving birth to a renewal in My Spirit Thrice Holy, surrendering Her to become

One; faint as your heart may be, feel, feel My joy for this victory! Salvation is at your doors ...! daughter, surrender into your Father's Hands; delicate and tender child, lift the yoke of Unity on your shoulders and carry it; when you weary on your way I will be your sole Repose, your sole Companion; in the betrayals, your sole Friend; I will be your sole Source of Knowledge, instructing you the depths of Our mysteries, so that this generation

40

and the next will not lack; I will continue to rain down on you My blessings and My Manna to feed you; come, do not stand in awe, come, your closeness to Me infatuates Me and renders your soul thirsty for Me; come, tabernacle of My Son, I love you; love Me and be eager to serve Me; come, dust and ashes, yet with a heart and soul, glorify Me; come Paraskevi, in contrast to your darkness I, who am the Imperishable Light of the Law, will be

41

your sole pillar of Light in your journey, to guide you and others into My Law; and you*, even if you are still struck with blindness, groping your way in this wilderness, lacking, starved and scorched dry, even if you feel conquered by bitter plague, return to Me as you are! for I have taken My stand against My Holy Wrath by reminding Myself that I, I had fathered you....

* From thereon God asked me to read this passage for the Scandinavian countries I visited: Oslo, Göteborg, Stockholm & Copenhagen.

42

and I will stand by you always and everywhere you go; approach the Living One and I will demonstrate My sweetness towards you, teaching you that piety is stronger than all; piety will keep you away from sin; come and strike your root in Me so that I turn you too, into a Tree with branches that bear fruit, and My inscription will be carved on each one of your fruits so that those who eat will hunger for more; and from thereon you will

43

tune your ear to the Truth thrice Holy; and by applying your heart to the Truth you shall live

27.9.95

My gaze is in the visions of the Night,
as swiftly as You, the Holy One,
came to me, so was Your swiftness
to throw Your veil over my eyes
for this is what pleased You, Beloved
of the Father, so that I may
depend on You entirely and be like
a toy in Your Mighty Hand.
And since then, I have become an exile for Your Sake.

It pleases You to trace out my path
so that You and I walk together,

44

I, clutching the hem of Your garment for fear of losing You and You, like a King amid His armies, You lead me where You choose.

And on our way, jealous men rise to their feet to interrupt our delightful journey, they lay their hands on me to rip me apart, but You, in a lordly style, lift my soul and carry it up to ride the wind with You, then You and I celebrate Your Strength; and in Your smiles, in Your childish joy and delight, we become accomplices and collaborators of our friendship.

You thwart the plans of our persecutors, while Your Mouth sings to me songs of deliverance. You open the door of Your Heart so that I step in and hide within Its depths.

45

My soul rejoices in the Lord.
He has the power to mould every heart by His faithful Love.
When my soul is downcast, You do not wait, but You show Your Love in Your eagerness to hearten me by embracing me.

Your glance, Delight of the Father, has every capacity to transform any soul to become from a tragic song into an inspired hymn.

Yes, Lord, in every way You can make Your people into a canticle, changing their rhythm, to preserve the tone of Your Voice, because You never disdain anyone, but stand by us always and everywhere.

46

My Delight, worship Me! you are in touch with Me, with My Spirit and with My Father; bring this work of Mercy We are giving you across the world together with your counsellor;

I do not want to fall into spiritual decay and drag my mission. I am in the Night!

never mind what is beyond your means*[1] and your strength for I will fill up what lacks; give Us as much as you can; did you not notice*[2]? though you

*[1] Means of understanding.
*[2] During my meetings in Holland and all Scandinavia.

47

are a nothing I was seen on you*[1]; in your distress I have been successful; in your great trials I overflowed My Treasures in many hearts; would I do these things*[2] to you if I did not love you? and I intend to continue keeping My veil on your eyes so that you will have no opportunity of grieving Me by becoming elated; these are the ways I treat My predilected souls into obedience and effacement; I am King and I govern

*[1] Jesus appeared in my place. His Face though was reported to have appeared beaten up.

*[2] Jesus means the trials He permits to come my way.

48

over them so that they reach the perfect goodness for the glory of Our Trinitarian Holiness ♡ and, as I once said to My disciples, I say to you too: 'now that you know this, happiness will be yours if you behave accordingly'* ♡ (Jn 13:1
your Jesus who loves you; ic

St Michael's feast-day - 29. 9. 95

have My Peace; it is I, Jesus; My Archangel, Saint Michael wants to be courteous to you, since you remembered

* In obedience and effacement like His predilected soul a total submission.

49

that it is His Feast Day, He will satisfy your good disposition ♡ ic

St. Michael speaks:

friend of Our Lord; I, Saint Michael greet you in the Name of Our Lord Most High ♡ do you know what is holding back ♡ the wrath of God Almighty?

No, I do not know...

I will tell you then, little souls! yes! little souls who persevere in prayer, fasting and penance... through these, many will be saved; ah, Vassula,

50

never cease praying the Rosary; never cease asking Me for My intercession; may honour and glory be given to God for His inexhaustible patience*; come, be confident and do not fall into temptation; see? it is not worth it.... listen and continue to listen to your Father in Heaven; God is not unattainable, He is at everyone's reach; so call your Abba and He will hear

* At this very moment I suddenly had for just two seconds a doubt, which left me almost immediately, and I burst into a great joy again when I said: " see? it is not worth it."

51

you ♡ the Most Holy Trinity wants everyone to reach and enter into the highest heaven; happy are those who die in the Lord, theirs is the Kingdom of heaven; fear God and always praise Him; worship your Maker and love Him always ♡ I, Saint Michael, the Archangel, bless you in the presence of the Most Holy Trinity and in the presence of Their Holy Angels;—

– Saint Michael – and while you are working, you can continue

52

praying! *

2. 10. 95

- Feast of our guardian angels. -

Alleluia!
Let heaven praise Yahweh:
praise Him, heavenly heights,
praise Him, all His angels,
praise Him, all His armies! (Ps 148, 1-2

Let them all praise the Name of Yahweh,
at whose command they were created.
(Ps 148, 5)

I, Jesus give you My Peace; come and pray with Me, say:

* I had to prepare our dinner, this is why St Michael said to pray while working.

53

Sovereign from the beginning,
hear My prayer;
my soul, my heart are thirsting
for you;
my gaze longs to see you, and
I look to no one else,
for there is no god to compare
You with,
nothing is greater than you,
since you alone are stupendously
great,
for this, gather the nations

54

to give thanks and praise
to Your Holy Name
around one single Tabernacle,
let them offer Your Sacrifice
together to Our Father
in heaven, in one voice and in
the same Spirit;
Guardian of our soul,
wonderfully strong, unconquerable,
may the whole of Your creation
serve You in the Most Holy Trinity;
grant us this blessing; amen —

come now, in the power of My Spirit I am sending you Daniel, your guardian angel ♡ ic

My angel speaks:

I, Dan, bless you, Sign of Unity*, remain faithful to the Lord; grow in Him and in no one else; alone Yahweh is good; pray to be fortified so that in the Lord you may draw strength to revive His House and accomplish

* At the same time I heard 'Sign', I also heard simultaneously the word: 'Symbol'.

56

your mission, I will always guard you, forever I shall guide you; your

Daniel

your guardian angel

guarding you;

Daniel

57

6. 10. 95

My Lord! My eyes were privileged to contemplate Your glorious Majesty; what grace have You given me! I, who am the least, to have received such a gift to be able to possess Your Majesty, and contemplate You in Your Mystery.

- Fountain of Wisdom, You are treating me in a supreme way, full of goodness and boundless tenderness to recognize my God Thrice Holy, to recognize Him as Father, as Beloved and Abba.

- Fountain of Understanding that makes gardens out of deserts, fruit-trees out of thorns and thistles, incredibly ravishing, palpitating, Your glorious appearance leaves my heart spellbound.

- Fountain of Counsel, my Cup, my Drink, King from the beginning,

58

You are continuously displaying Your Majestic counsel with kindness to your pupil; this is why my heart is pining away with love.

Glory is His Holy Name; how can one praise You enough?

- Fountain of Fortitude, resplendently awesome, have You seen how we are? Reduced, lacking, weak, and a deplorable sight, yet, we belong to You, we come from You. See? see how our knees are trembling and are weak for lack of Food? See how so many of us have become an object of derision?

So come, Spirit of Grace, I implore Your Majesty to put Your Breath once more in us so that fresh life begins. One Word of command from You and the entire

59

world can be renewed!

- O Fountain of Knowledge, come and govern me to penetrate the Mystery of God; my eyes have seen nothing, my ears have heard nothing and my touch will still remain in the unknown, unless You show me Your Face, and let me hear Your Voice; have You not noticed how I yearn for Your Courts?

- Fountain of Piety, why is it so difficult to grasp You? Is it because my hands are so soiled? Why do you shy away from me? Am I to remain imperfect? You are always true to Your promises, and You are known to give liberty to prisoners, and so I invoke You, grant me the attitude of Your Saints so that I may celebrate Your acts of power one day. Liberate me, for under Your protection the pious are known to be safe.

Fountain of Fear, token of Your true disciples, pearl of Your Kingdom, heart-beat of the Church and reverence to Its Mysteries, how can we obtain You and possess You eternally? You are all .... Rose-bud of my heart, grant me this gift so that I may be counted as one of Your daughters. To fear You is the root of all wisdom and the entrance of eternal Life.

O Glorious Throne, set high from the beginning, uproot me from all evil and show me the One sitting on You!

I* shall pour on you and anyone who desires Me My Light thrice Holy; to save you and bring you in your Father's Home; I will fill your spirit with My

*The Holy Spirit speaks.

61

Breath; you are frailly rooted still, but count Me as your dearest Friend who will preserve you from being uprooted; when you walk, delightful child, I will be your sole Guide, when you lie down, your faithful Watchman, when you wake, your cheerful Companion; [*1] peace be with you; have you not read: "do not refuse a kindness to anyone who begs it, if it is in your power to perform it;"[*2] so I said: "Vassiliki,

[*1] Jesus now speaks [*2] Pr. 3:27

62

whom My Spirit bound to Me in matrimonial bonds and whom I reared, you shall enjoy My favour, you shall enjoy My Presence; this is why I came out to meet you, and I tell you, daughter I am content as a child that has been weaned; My happiness is complete; remain faithful to Me, remember I am your Spouse, try then to imitate your Spouse, even to assume the condition of a slave... daughter, night and day My Name is blasphemed and I am injured by My

63

Own sons and daughters, - I am persecuted - share in My sufferings, I am reduced to beg for your love; I am reduced to beg for your generosity; share in My sufferings; tonight many of My victim souls will unburden Me ....

Lord! it looks as if things have gone out of hand!

do not mourn for Me but for this generation .... I love you to folly and I would go back to Calvary any time again if this were possible to save you

64

from this Apostasy; I need generosity and warmth, a proof of love .... I tell you, daughter, I do not regret coming to you; yes, I have seen how this generation is reduced and lacking; and My Sacred Heart pains Me beyond human comprehension this is why, My Vassula, I want you to fan into a flame all that I have given you, all those Treasures of My Heart, they are meant to be distributed; you have been trusted to look after this Inexhaustible Treasure I had been reserving

Excerpts from Notebook 81

6 October 95, continued from NB #80, p.64...I intend to gather you all like lambs and show you your place of rest

✠ The beast today challenges Heaven, even My Power!

✠ By the word of My Mouth and the command of My Father, the present sky and earth are destined for fire

13 October 95 (Tucuman), NB p. 5...I have adopted Vassula...watch over her with the same eyes I watch over her

✠ I beg you, do not use any harshness in any way

17 October 95, NB p.9...Your new birth is not from mortal seed but from my Spirit

25 October 95, NB p.12...<u>You yourself keep My silence</u>, you have enough witnesses who could defend you

✠ While your oppressors will be rejoicing, My seventh angel will empty his bowl into the air igniting the whole atmosphere into fire

8 November 95, NB p.16... I am from Heaven and no creature will be able to overpower Me in you

✠ You and I are nearing the tenth anniversary of "True Life In God"

10 November 95, NB p.23...I have raised you to be My powerful Sign of rejection; the rejection of My Love

✠ My father's Lips brim with fury for the unrepentant sinners

15 November 95, NB p.31...Can you obey Me to the letter?

✠ They will hide the lamp I have given them and will hide in darkness so as not to be seen, by calling this darkness: 'prudence'

21 November 95, NB p.34...The three foul spirits <u>forming a triangle</u>...dragon and beast and false prophet

✠ In your nothingness I shall reveal My Power and overturn their kingdoms

28 November 95 (Anniversary of 10 years of "True Life in God"), NB p.38 ...You have become a part of Me, and I part of You

✠ By adopting you, I adopted so many others

1 December 95, NB p.45...You will see then the things that no eye has seen and no ear has heard

- ✠ My Spirit of Understanding…revealing to you that the Church, which is His Body on earth, fills the whole creation
- ✠ My Spirit of Counsel will…counsel your spirit to become a child
- ✠ I shall count you too as one of My children who reflect My Image
- ✠ Ask My Spirit of Fortitude to give you a warrior's heart, to fight the good fight of faith and justice
- ✠ Ask Our Trinitarian Holiness for the Spirit of Knowledge…of how to possess Me, your God
- ✠ If you look for My Spirit of Piety, you will be free to serve Me in a new spiritual way
- ✠ To fear Me is the root of the tree of Life

10 December 95, NB p.58...The world can offer you nothing that belongs to Me

- ✠ Everything I have said in this message is written in scriptures, but you have not understood yet fully what is written
- ✠ I will send you My Holy Spirit in full force on <u>all</u> mankind…I will display portents in heaven as never before; <u>there will be a second Pentecost</u>
- ✠ It is not for anyone to know times or dates
- ✠ Learn that I shall complete My Work triumphant
- ✠ My words have not found a home with them, no, because love is missing

for your times; distribute It with the help of My Holy Spirit; He who saved you will save others too; ♡ your Cup and your Drink will show Mercy to many of you for I intend to gather you all like lambs and show you all your place of rest ♡ as for your requests, I intend to send you My Holy Spirit from above so that a light may shine in your darkness; come, you who desire Me and feed yourself on My Word; My Word is wealth and your soul then

2

will array itself in My Magnificence;
Love is with you now and forever ....

Adorn, Lord, Your creation in Your magnificence.

I will put Peace in their heart and Salvation in their soul too if I hear from them a cry of repentance .... repent and you will obtain the fruit of pardon, forgive and you will obtain the fruit of love and peace; come and repent .... My Father's wrath has kindled a Fire that will burn the world up!

3

you see, daughter, this generation has planned to commit the abomination which My prophet, Daniel, spoke of; it will do a deed of horror; how can My Father not flare up? My Father will not bear the sight of His Son trampled underfoot, flung to the ground, nor will Saint Michael - Saint Michael and His armies will stand up; - the Beast today challenges Heaven, even My Power! this is why My Father will burn the crimes of this generation with Fire and this Fire

4

will come at a time when they suspect nothing: by the word of My Mouth and the command of My Father, the present sky and earth are destined for fire;

you have been warned about this many times, but instead of announcing you have been denouncing! .... mastered by your weakness*[1].... I tell you as Scriptures say: "*[2] happy those whose crimes are forgiven, whose sins are blotted out

*[1] Jesus said this as if speaking to Himself.
*[2] Rm 4:7 Ps. 32: 1-2

5

happy the man whom the Lord considers sinless" when My Day comes;
pray, My daughter, for your generation; persevere and I shall bring you Hope;
I bless you ♡ ic

Tucuman 13. 10. 95

Jesus?

I Am, allow Me to use your mouth; I shall remind them of My Love; — My precious one, tell your counsellor: because I laid down My Life voluntarily, My disciples were scandalized;

6

I laid It down of My Own free Will, but they failed to see yet that I had the power to take My Life up again; I allowed Myself to be suppressed for the sake of My sheep .... I have told you this so that your understanding may be complete*; as you know, I have adopted Vassula, so that in her I may be glorified and as I had sent others before her into the world, I am sending her now into

* It was about how to understand the word "suppress" in a previous message.

7

this world imbued in iniquity; her journey will not be easy*, because the Father wished it that way for His greatest glory; watch over her with the same eyes I watch over her; may your union reach the perfection I desire from you, do not let it decay; love one another as I love you; I beg you, do not use any harshness in any way, My friend, for this grieves My Holy Spirit; I am

* I heard also (at the same time) "is not easy."

8

gentle and My education is gentle; you will continue this journey together, through the nations I choose; — I am with you; be constant in your love and holiness; let My children enjoy the light that I am giving them through these Messages; continue, My friend, to honour Us in Our Trinitarian Holiness and to honour the Immaculate Heart of your Mother; in all truth I tell you: put into full action the Messages of Our Trinitarian Holiness and complete

9

your work; lean on Me and ask My Spirit to help you complete what you have commenced*; I bless you; I <u>am</u> with you; IC

17.10.95

My Lord and my Shepherd guide us,
straighten our paths;
we are the flock of Your sheepfold,
and I am confident, because of Your
Faithful Love, that You will fetch
the strayed sheep one after the other,
back into Your fold.

It was You my Shepherd, who drew me
from the entrails of this vile world.
Blessed be Your Name, thrice Holy.

Refreshment of my soul,
Perfect Beauty, with words

* The books

sweeter than honey,
open Your Mouth and pronounce
the Wonders of Your Law,
so that many will be set free.

Let Your faithful Love come
to all Your creation,
be gracious, generous and merciful
with us so that our eyes
will open and fix our gaze
on Your Trinitarian Holiness.
Amen

I, Jesus bless you; take My Mighty Hand,
I will guide you; to guide you and
to be your Holy Companion in the journey
of your life is a constant delight for
Me; see? I have given you the

freedom of heart; through My Spirit you get your freedom; through His purifying Fire you are washed clean; where My Spirit is, there is freedom, for there is a renewal, a transfiguration in His Presence; your new birth is not from mortal seed but from My Spirit; Joy-of-My-Heart, allow Me to use you as My net so that I may bring many hearts to live in this freedom; love Me and console Me; I am with you; glorify Me and bless My Holy Name thrice Holy; ΙΧΘΥΣ

12

25. 10. 95

peace be with you! I am with you; see how My predictions come true?* flower-of-My-Heart, flame-of-My-Eyes, your mission will be accomplished only when I will allow them to crucify you; now you are travelling by a rough road but I am with you; take courage and do not lose the Peace I have given you; I had told you that the Father had traced

* Messages foretelling, are many, but here are some:

13

for you a road similar to Mine; what I had succumbed you would succumb too but all would be in accordance and to the measure of your strength; today as you see, you have been sold by one of My Own; precious one, your own people have betrayed innocent blood .... you were handed over by one of your own*[1] to the Romans so that they condemn you and then ... be crucified; Vassula, you yourself keep My silence,*[2] you have enough

*[1] Christ made me understand who. *[2] I should not defend myself.

14

witnesses who could defend you; the faithful will remain faithful; your clothes, My child, will roll in your blood, and this, too, will be the evidence that you come from Me; you were born for this and your acceptance delights Me because through your sufferings I will save many; through your torments I will be setting light inside My Church, giving birth to a renewal in My Holy Spirit thrice Holy; in the meantime while your oppressors will be rejoicing, My seventh

15

angel will empty his bowl into the air, igniting the whole atmosphere into fire*[1]... Vassiliki, look at Me, in the Eyes*[2]... you will promise Me, if you love Me, to forgive them all, it may sound illogical to many but you are My follower, are you not?

yes, Lord.

copy then your Master, for in the end I shall triumph.... till this

*[1] A reminder of Akita's message in Japan

*[2] I did and I melted.

16

moment they are failing to understand that this Message comes from Me*....

I thank You, my Lord,
for all that You are doing for me,
I love You even more!

My dove, your Saviour loves you and blesses you; ic

8. 11. 95

Lord, King, from the beginning
and Master of all things,
I am flesh of Your Flesh,
bone of Your Bone,
You are in me and I am in You,
What joy, what delight
to know that I possess You and

* Jesus was speaking like to himself, in a lower voice.

17

that You possess me!
I belong to You and You, my
King, belong to me!

You are the true Vine and
I am one of Your branches,
I am Your remnant,
what a joy to be one with You!
And I intend to remain in You
so that You remain in me.
O what a gift from Your Spirit!
Allelluya!

Lay down Your Plans, O Lord,
and I will take anything
You offer me, now I am being bold,
but is it suffering You want of me?
I will take anything You give me,
everything becomes so beautiful when
it comes from You!
Come! Come and reign in me
You are the Source of my happiness!
Are You inviting me to share Your Cup?

18

A Cup where Your Divine Lips sipped from?
My God! my God I tremble with emotion and delight;
O Love! You have seduced me!

My Own Heart swells with emotion, to have invited Me at your table in this way .... trust Me, I am from Heaven and no creature will be able to overpower Me in you; I am well alive in you; no one living in the worldly kingdoms and the one* who reigns over them will be able to topple My Reign in you;

* Satan

19

I am God thrice holy so do not fear; remember what I have told you once? I have told you that I am known to overthrow kings and kingdoms were they to become an obstacle on My way; all I ask from you now is fidelity; remain faithful to Me; do not look to your left nor to your right; I will help you; rejoice My friend for I have honoured you by inviting you to share My Cup, the Cup of your division and the insincerity of your hearts .... now, you and I are

20

nearing the tenth anniversary of 'True Life in God', take courage, My daughter, and do not get offended when the world* deprives you of honours; dwell in perpetual discipline towards My Church and you will enjoy My favour, be always ready to respond to My calls by saying: "here I am, Lord," and your Creator shall shine on you; My Father's Choice, do not fall into temptation, learn where knowledge is to be found, where perseverance, where wisdom are and

* Several newspapers calumniated me.

21

life; in your silence you will find all these things and more, in My Holy Spirit; enjoy moving in My Spirit, like a fish in water; out of this water, you will die and dry up; so remain in My Spirit and breathe in My Spirit and you will live; be happy! I have nursed you and reared you to bring to Me hoards of souls; many of them are still unwilling to return to Me .... how I pity them! I am in agony and suffering to see them so totally unaware of the dangers surround-

22

ing them; ah ... Vassula, join Me in My sufferings, join Me in My agonies, console Me and rest Me ....

I love You, Lord, what can I do more?

love Me, this consoles Me; — ahead of you, serpents may be wanting to strike and are waiting for you; but although they have taken a transparency so that one cannot spot them immediately, I will give you eyes to see them; do not fear, for I am with you, not one of them will be able to strike you; in the end one serpent will swallow the other!* yes! like in the vision I gave you; come, I love you and bless you ♡ ΙΧΘΥΣ 

10. 11. 95

Glory be to God in the highest heaven,
Glory be to Him who lifted my soul
from the entrails of this earth;
Glory be to the Light thrice Holy in whose
power all things came to be;
Glory be to God, invincible, incomparable in His Authority;
Glory be to the Immortal One in whom
we find immortality;
May Your Breath Most Holy One
which is pure emanation of Your Glory,
enliven us, renewing us into
one glorious Body.

Amen.

* Like in my vision of 29.1.89

24

peace; My child, listen: those who treat you ruthlessly today will have to face Me one day and give Me their accounts.... they will not venture to say then: "what have we done wrong?" because I shall show them the impressive wounds their arrogance did to My Body, and according to the scourge I receive daily from them will I sentence them .... they will be given ten times the amount; My child, likeness to My Image, you are indeed the most tormented messenger

25

on earth, but also the most privileged; I have privileged you with My Thorned Crown, My Nails and My Cross; I have raised you to be My powerful Sign of rejection; the rejection of My Love.... ah, so many of you are locked in the same sleep.... — listen, Vassula, I will tell you a small secret: in these days of ordeal for you, I have attracted many souls to My Heart and I have also liberated many souls from purgatory who were bound for many years!

26

see? nothing goes in vain; ah! My Heart is like on fire now, for through your sufferings I can do great things! My children are not expiating as I want them to, so on you My Eyes fell, knowing that you will not refuse your Saviour's supplications and that you will allow yourself to be crushed by those who cry out for justice and peace yet do just the opposite; let the whole world now rejoice and believe they have conquered 'bitter plague'; let them believe they have

27

silenced you; yes, a multitude will rise to strike you down, as a multitude had risen to strike Me down and have Me crucified; many false witnesses will appear in the last minute testifying falsely on you, as so many rose to testify falsely on your Saviour; indeed, they will violently press their accusations on innocent blood, see? what they have done to Me will be done to you but within the measure your soul can take; mockery will continue by trumpeting low and high that you are a false prophet, as when My guards mocked Me by beating Me, blindfolding Me then striking Me in turn and asking Me: "play the prophet, who hit you?" you will appear as the loser before the eyes of the world, as I, your Lord, appeared on My Cross; all these things will come on your way so that the Father's words be accomplished; – I am the Resurrection and I will raise up all that I have written through your hand, so that everyone may believe that 'True Life in God' was not written by

flesh but by the Spirit of Grace; darkness and distress should not be felt by you, for I have hidden you into My Sacred Heart; — My little soul, let My Majestic Voice be heard and do not be frightened by the noise there is around you;
My Father's Lips brim with fury for the unrepentant sinners and His anger will be displayed by a glare of a devouring fire; why, He announced it not long ago, by your Mother, to Akita's*

* In Japan

30

messenger*; in the end, the earth will open its ears and heart so that salvation springs up, and I will triumph together with the Immaculate Heart of your and My Mother; — vessel of My agonies, I will give you enough strength to accomplish your mission with dignity that will glorify Me; My Love for you covers you so do not fear, 'lo tedhal'.... I, Jesus Christ, am with you now and always ♡ ΙΧΘΥΣ

* Sister Agnès.

31

15. 11. 95

Scriptures say: "..the ear is a judge of speeches, just as the palate can tell one food from another." (Jb 34:3) How is it they have not discovered Your Speech, how is it that Your Food was not appreciated or tasty for them? How is it that Scriptures are rejected in my case? When the Jews accused You, Jesus, and did not believe You were sent by God, and that You are God's Son and God Yourself, You said to them: "I have done many good works for you to see, works from my Father; for which of these are you stoning me? .... If I am not doing my Father's work, there is no need to believe me; but if I am doing it, then even if you refuse to believe in me, at least believe in the work I do." - Why then, Lord, do they not look at the works done in Your Name, are these not my witness?

peace be with you; Love is with you;

32

can you obey Me to the letter? I wish that this trial will not cause you to lose My Peace; I am the Author of this Message, so do not give up; I will rescue you; am I not allowed to test you and all the others? am I not allowed to strengthen you through trials? (Vassula, I will send you an angel to console you.... you call out to Me: "Lord, I am badly wounded," but, Vassula, so am I. you cry out: "Lord, I am brutally treated," and I am telling you, but so am I ; — My chosen one has been struck from inside My House and this was so that what the Father had said to you, would be accomplished .... and now I tell you, if any sacerdotal soul declares openly himself for Me* in the presence of the world, I will too, when the time comes, declare Myself for him in the presence of My Father! — and to you I tell you: do not defend yourself! let those who heard you testify now and openly declare

* Jesus talks about His Message

34

the truth; but the devil will silence some of them by sending them a dumb spirit; they will hide the lamp I have given them and will hide in darkness so as not to be seen, by calling this darkness: 'prudence'; ic

21. 11. 95

Have I toiled in vain? Have I exhausted myself for nothing? Yet all the while my course was with You. My charism is given by You, my God, this is why You were my Strength.

My Vassula, why do you say, 'were my Strength?' why do you talk in 'the past? you are under My service still and you are permanently strengthened by Me; I am still your Strength and will always be ....

no, you have not laboured in vain nor have you been spent for nothing; your abandonment has done prodigies in My Spirit; is a country born in one day? likewise nor is it possible that unity be born in one single day since many of My elect follow their own ways; a Voice was sent to the nations to speak and console My children, to turn them

36

back to Me; I provided seeds to be sown in the field of reconciliation and I had provided you with My spiritual bread so that My Word fills those who lacked;

– your race, Vassula, is not over because I have created you to be My weapon against the Destroyer who renders many of My people blind; you will have nothing to fear since I am with you .... yes, the Destroyer captivated their mind by its power over the world and its name lies in Scriptures as the three foul spirits forming

37

<u>a triangle</u>; those three foul spirits coming from the jaws of dragon and beast and false prophet,* why, they have awakened with your sound since you are My Echo and <u>so have sworn, by overturning My Chalice, to silence you</u>; they have sworn to surge over you and against you; My little angel, in your frailty I shall disarm the mighty ones; in your nothingness I shall reveal My Power and overturn their kingdoms; take courage,

* Ap. 16:13 ²*

38

daughter, and I will re-establish the truth; I bless you; ΙΧΘΥΣ 

Anniversary of 10 years 28. 11. 95
of True Life in God

peace be with you; My Vassula, ah, let Me know, let Me know, are you happy to have been with Me in this way all these years? mere creature of flesh, but with a heart, are you happy?

Crown-of-my-Joy, how could I not be happy? I have been carried off by Your Breath in the clouds to advance on the wings of the wind, to become a part of the winds*, so how can I not be happy!

* "You use the winds as messengers." Ps 104: 4

39

and you have become part of Me*, and I part of you, and you have made your home in Me, as I have made My Home in you, transfiguring your soul into an Eden so that I may be glorified; advance your step and go forward on the wings of the wind, for you have a special place in My Sacred Heart;

Feast-of-my-own-heart! Ointment-of-my-eyes! Light thrice Holy! my soul rejoices because You have rescued the

* Allusion to Jn 15

40

'Uninhabited'; blessed be Your Name thrice Holy;

indeed if I am your 'Feast-of-your-own heart,' celebrate annually the date of today where I brought you and so many others to come into My Heart ♡ and discover those innumerable treasures I kept for your times; keep this great day in mind; be by My side as you have been for the past ten years now: NEVER leave My side, walk with Me as you have done all these years; see

41

how I educated you? see what I have accomplished? see My Wisdom? by adopting you, I adopted so many others; My path is straight, My ways of approaching you are delightful.... your King is perfect and beautiful; "revive My Church, embellish My Church, unite My Church", was My Order to you, and all I asked from you, to be able to work with you for My glory, was for you to consent to do My Will; and so you have won My friendship, My Church benefits now

42

from so many souls who returned to Me.... and now their praises to Me are joined with those of My angels in heaven; and from your mouth I spoke, giving what My Heart desires most for Unity; you have not toiled in vain; I had asked you to pass on My Words and My desire: the unification of the date of Easter, and so you have; see? to have acknowledged Me, My child, was indeed the perfect virtue and the light of your soul; daughter from Egypt, I kept guard on you constanby, the twilight I longed for in your soul was given to you by My Spirit thrice Holy, to fulfil My whole purpose; — My words: "full, you shall be many," were an enigma to you; then I made you understand what they meant: "when you shall be filled with My Holy Spirit, thrice Holy and giver of life, you shall, with the power of My Spirit, convert and bring to repentance many." I have cultivated your soil with My Own Hand, and shattered the rocks to level My way

44

in you; then I have sown My Own celestial seeds in you; to honour My Name, I vowed to knock down any intruder who would come My way into My new garden; night and day I delighted watching over you; today I can say, Vassula: I have not toiled in you for nothing; My Spirit set you free so that you would be a proper place to be lived in by Me ♡ may My sons and daughters approach Me and I shall free them to join My assembly too ♡ IΧΘΥΣ

45

1.12.95

I hallow Your Holy Name,
while I still stand in awe
before Your Glory.

The Spirit of above invites me,
telling me that to fear You*[1]
my God is a treasure given
by Wisdom Herself.

*[2] and My Reign begins in you then, followed by My Spirit of Understanding, to assure you of your Father's Divinity, thrice Holy, My Spirit will establish your foundations in the Truth by revealing to your spirit what the sages and your philosophers call foolish and nonsense. He will en-

*[1] "The fear of Yahweh is His Breath" (Is. 11:2)
*[2] The Eternal Father speaks.

46

lighten the eyes of your mind, giving you a spirit of perception, infinitely rich, to penetrate into the full mystery of Our Divinity you will see then the things that no eye has seen and no ear has heard, things beyond the mind of man, because your mind will have been stamped with the seal of My Holy Spirit, and all things that seemed impenetrable and unattainable for your spirit to understand will be understood in Our Divine Light, and I, together with My Spirit of Understanding, will make

47

your mind like the mind of My Son, Jesus Christ; then, fully in the Truth, your spirit will reach the fullness of Christ Himself revealing to you that the Church, which is His Body on earth, fills the whole creation; O what would I not Counsel you! your aim must be to remain in the Truth; for this your spirit should be dedicated to the Holy Trinity; My Spirit of Counsel will help you live a saintly life because your only joy will be for you to abide by My Law, blessed and thrice

48

Holy it is; He will counsel your spirit to become a child, innocent, to run to Me, then have a heart-to-heart conversation, showing Me no distrust, and I shall count you, too, as one of My children who reflect My Image; the light then in your eyes will be the Light of My Son, Jesus Christ, and you will be assigned a place among the saints; find Me in simplicity of heart, and fasten your heart on holiness, integrity and love; thirst for Me your God, and the barriers to reach Me will be

49

broken by your love; in your sight then will appear the One whom your soul languished for, dearer to you than all the riches of the world and your own life, the Blessed and only Ruler of all, the Unique, Trinitarian yet One in the unity of essence, the Irresistible and Glorious, the Incomparable One, to welcome you into His Kingdom; ask for My Spirit of Counsel so that you do not swerve from the Truth ♡ be determined to obtain from My Spirit of Fortitude strength to be able to resist

50

temptations that come your way; and to overcome with courage and stability any obstacle that can deprive you of My Imperishable Light; ask My Spirit of Fortitude to give you a warrior's heart, to fight the good fight of faith and justice and join in this spiritual battle of My Archangels Michael and Raphael, predominant in strength and valiant, Warriors of Justice, observing through the light of My Holy Spirit, every aspect of human behaviour; open your mouth and ask!

51

He who lives forever and who created all the universe tells you: open your mouth, ask and I shall hear you; the day of visitation is at hand, humble yourself and ask for My Spirit of Fortitude to give you the power and strength to carry your cross with dignity and fervour so that through your pains and your generosity you will become partners of My Son Jesus Christ's triumph, be confident and come and ask Our Trinitarian Holiness for the Spirit of Knowledge, the Knowledge of how to

52

possess Me your God, the Knowledge of approaching Me in footsteps as those of My angels; if your lands are set aflame it is because of your so little knowledge of who I Am; yes, wickedness burns like a fire; come! you who err aimlessly in rounds and are so naked and pitiful to look at, come to Me and ask, by a simple utterance, the Spirit of Knowledge, and I shall send Him to you, and when He comes He will show you how you had ceased to be. no sooner born .... and although you appeared to be, you were dead long ago and the stench of your death had reached My nostrils; My Spirit will teach you to know yourself and to listen to My Calls; and when you do, a light will shine inside you revealing Me, your Triune God, in all My Glory, loving to man, Incomparable, Just and Holy; how is it that so few ask for My Spirit of Piety? is it your pride of heart that stops you? have you ever attempted to understand how you move and how everything created moves in My

54

Spirit thrice Holy? if you look for My Spirit of Piety, you will be free to serve Me in a new spiritual way, renouncing your spirit of lethargy that had encamped in you making a gulf between you and Me; how have you been so slow to ask for the Spirit of Piety, to teach you the knowledge of all holy things, and that piety is stronger in submissiveness, in humility, and in renunciation; ask! ask and I shall despatch My Spirit from above to come and rest

55

on you, so that henceforth you will become the delight of My Eyes and the flame of My Son's Eyes, the starlight of your surrounding, which is so dark and in your radiance the attraction of your so corrupt society, attracting them to Me; in your radiance you will radiate My Son, Jesus Christ's Image; and I shall fill your hands with outnumbered riches to delight My Soul while serving Me, your Triune God, yet One, in the essence of unity ♡ from thereon

56

you will dread to displease Me, for in you I shall place My Spirit of Fear; every time you will come to Me you will come and kneel before My Majesty, in awe, since your spirit would have tasted the fruits of My Wisdom; to fear Me is the crown of Wisdom; to fear Me is the root of the tree of life; come and breathe in My Spirit, come and move in My Spirit; and I will reveal to you in the innermost part of your heart the depths of Myself so that you, too, may possess Me ♡ the Spirit from above invites you all to penetrate into the mystery of the seven Gifts of My Holy Spirit; come and be blessed; come and let there be light in your soul; the invisible things are eternal; come and obtain what is invisible from the Spirit, so that you may live with Us and be one in Us ♡

58

10.12.95

peace be with you; your aim must be to remain in the Truth and draw all people to the Truth and into My Kingdom; I am the Truth and My Kingdom on earth is My Church and My Church is My Body which fills the whole creation*; and the Life of My Church is My Holy Eucharist, the Way to eternal life; — I am the Way, the Truth and the Life; I am Love, love Me and you shall live; through love your soul will begin to look

* Eph 1:23

59

for heavenly things; the world can offer you nothing that belongs to Me; cling to Me and you will remain rooted in Me and in this way you will win for yourself the eternal life which I promised you; I have called you, My Vassula, and I have taken you to draw, through My Call, many sinners for repentance; in the presence of many witnesses I spoke through you, appearing in your place; some have seen Me and believed; happy are those who have not seen and yet believe; I have

60

indeed entrusted you with this Message, because I knew you would take good care of My Interests; I said, I have entrusted you with this Message, this Message adds nothing new to Scriptures; everything I have said in this Message is written in Scriptures, but you have not understood yet fully what is written; you heard Me say: I will send you the Paraklétos to be with you for ever and in those who love Me to teach you everything; My Spirit will be your Counsellor and your

61

Educator; without Him even My Disciples never fully understood Me nor My teachings; but on that day I returned to the Father, I sent the Paraklētos to them so that He reminds them of everything I had said to them while I was with them; I am all prepared now to come to you, but you have still not understood how and in which way; yet I have not been speaking in metaphors; I tell you solemnly: I will send you My Holy Spirit in full force on all mankind, and as a foresign I will display portents in heaven as

62

never before; <u>there will be a second Pentecost</u> so that My Kingdom on earth* will be restored; many of you ask: 'when? when will all these things take place?' it is not for anyone to know times or dates that the Father has decided by His own authority; - in the past your ancestors killed all those who foretold My Coming; and now, in your generation, you are doing the same; for how long are you to resist My Holy Spirit of Grace? repent

* Jesus means the Church.

63

of this wickedness of yours and pray so that none of the things you have spoken may condemn you; doubt no longer, you will soon receive an outpouring of My Holy Spirit so that your strength may be brought back;

and you, sister of Mine, receive the tenderness of He who formed you; where you failed I succeeded; where you lacked, My Holy Spirit replenished; My sympathy for you is immense; continue to put into action the lessons learnt from Me; learn that I shall complete My Work triumphant;

64

Vassula, will you go with Me just a mile longer?

Ofcourse, if I still have my feet on me to walk with You.

their severe treatment of you will not affect you; My Message has been revealed to My saints and to those with a child's heart; Wisdom shuns from the wise and the learned, but all those who have raised their sword against you shall perish by the sword; My Words have not found a home with them, no, because love is missing.....

Excerpts from Notebook 82

10 December 95, continued from NB 81, p.64...Go where I am sending you, go as a witness and proclaim openly

13 December 95, NB p.3...Do not be tempted to produce your own defence

- ✠ Dwell in perpetual discipline towards My Church and you will enjoy my favour
- ✠ I have revealed to My Church, through you, the Evil one's plans

3 January 96, NB p.7...I shall not fail you, so do not fail Me either

- ✠ Your mouth will be like a sword to all those who are wreaking havoc in My Sanctuary
- ✠ My Eyes favour the little hearts

9 January 96, NB p.14...My Holy Spirit is hardly remembered, proclaimed or relied on

- ✠ Do you think your prophecies came out of yourself, My child?
- ✠ I will let the wind carry My Breath to them sooner than I had planned
- ✠ Many of you will be singing in tongues; others will have the eloquence of speech
- ✠ I am offering you an Inestimable Treasure more beautiful than any man could conceive of obtaining
- ✠ Why, why do you ask from Me so very little...and with so little faith?
- ✠ The interior Intercessor within you...lifts your spirit...and brings you in communion with My Saints and My Angels

27 January 96, NB p.28...All the words I whisper in your ear are life

- ✠ I am your Father before your earthly father
- ✠ Obey My principles but with a heart and not a rock
- ✠ Honour the Woman adorned with the sun! ...Find your comfort...in those same arms that carried My Son...into Egypt

✠ I take no pleasure in your comments combined with sneers on the Woman so highly favoured by Me and to each I will pay his due

30 January 96, NB p.38...Break into joyful cries

✠ I will not allow them to give you more than what is necessary

✠ They shed innocent blood and their hands are covered with this blood

31 January 96, NB p.43...My Father stood up, His cry echoing in every heavenly ear

✠ Do you want to prolong your sufferings, My child on earth, or do you want to wake up in the morning in My Light

✠ What shall I do when My Father stands up again?

✠ All that you do, do so in a spirit of gentleness, even if your testimony is not accepted, be in peace

✠ The times are evil, but remember, your Creator leans tenderly over you all

12 February 96, NB p.57...When Cardinal will go against Cardinal, bishop against bishop, priest against priest

✠ My branch, do not worry as long as you are part of the true Vine and bear fruit

✠ My Love is in your heart to console you; come

18 March 96, NB p.63...You shall walk, you shall talk, you shall move hearts, you shall cast out devils...and you shall plant goodness

✠ Even after your death, your body will keep prophesying

doctors of the law they call themselves .... which law? Mine or theirs? had they kept My Law they would have understood My language*; but they do not take in what I said; ah, Vassula, repay evil with love, forgive and keep My silence to any blame thrust on you; a man draws on his own store, so honour Me since you come from Me; go where I am sending you, go as a witness and proclaim openly all that the Father and I have taught you;

* Jesus means in the Scriptures.

2

Satan's hour is here, but soon Saint Michael will stand up and woe to the unrepentant sinner! now the devil is vomiting his rage over you and over every one of My interventions for your salvation, the sting of iniquity, but My Holy Spirit will come to your rescue and My Message will become a continuous canticle to the ears who want to hear; pray, My Vassula, for your prayers delight Me; I bless you;

ΙΧΘΥΣ 

3

13. 12. 95

With great frenzy they are trying to wall me in. They want to shut my prayers to You. They have distorted Your words and now they are determined to obstruct my path.

My Vassula, peace be with you; have I not predicted this from the beginning so that you may know it? do not be tempted to produce your own defence; your witnesses will defend you; their works of siege are nothingness; trust Me; soon you will have to depart .... as for the walls they are building to wall you in, My Spirit will blow them down; and I will show My Glory

4

through you if you remain faithful to Me; now they say: "ah.... now we have swallowed her up;" what they do not know and they do not observe is My Wisdom; as for you, My child, dwell in perpetual discipline towards My Church and you will enjoy My favour; in these days, I have revealed to My Church, through you, the Evil one's plans; so aflame with anger Satan, who is the prince of this world, is well on his way to overpower all My Works; he was a murderer from the beginning,

5

and his aim is especially on My sacerdotal souls; he roams around to steal and bring to damnation My very Own .... it is in My power to reverse your situation, Vassula, but as you know, a servant is not greater than his master; I am your Master and since the authorities persecuted your Master, I allow them to persecute you, too; but 'lo tedhal'* I am with you; I am going to be your drink, your food, your rest, your peace and your joy; see? pray

* 'Do not fear' in Aramaic.

6

and adore Me; pray and follow Me;

ic

(Together with a hermit- Bethlehem -) 16. 12. 95

My Saviour, we put our whole heart into following You, into fearing You and seeking Your Face once more.
Do not disappoint us! Dn 3:23(41)

have My Peace; please Me and say these words:

Jesus, my only love,
Jesus, my inspiration,
my soul's companion,
Jesus,
You alone are my cup,

7

my drink, my blessing,
hide me in the core of your Heart
until death will deliver me in heaven;
Guardian of my soul,
be with me wherever I go ♡

amen;

let this be your theme; I blessed you and bless you again; Love is with you; we, us?

ic –

3. 1. 96

Yahweh, Your Works are blessings,
wealth and a Lamp.

8

Forgive us* for not accepting Them as from You with all our heart.

My daughter, I, your Father, give you My Peace; from the dawn of your earliest days I made you sit in My Court to teach you: righteousness, love, and who I Am; so that you do not adopt the ways of the world, I descended on you to conquer your heart; I wanted you to become My

* If I say "us", it is because I belong to the same family that God created and I beseech pardon on behalf of my family who do not believe still that these messages come from God.

9

friend and teach you that to fear Me is the beginning of Wisdom; although you did not deserve to see My Glory, I came to you in your silence, to obtain your 'yes'; I then commanded darkness not to be dark around you and that night would transform itself into light; member of the Eastern House, daughter of this House, false witnesses have risen against you but put your hope in Me, your Father; keep My instructions and be at peace and do not be worn out; endure and proclaim My

10

Glory and My Fatherly Call; in the Courts of My House you will remain to progress and progress My people; I shall not fail you, so do not fail Me either; I tell you: once the oppression is over and the ruler of the underworld chained and those who trample My Son's Sacrifice underfoot gone away, from within the House you are in, a man of good omen will stand up, flaring like a torch to restore My Sanctuary and My Name thrice Holy .... and the Rebel's kingdom shall fall; I shall continue to

"

be your Song, My Vassula, and your Torch; I shall be by your side and lead you safely all the days of your life; you shall be My collaborator and My friend, My echo and My weapon; and your mouth will be like a sword to all those who are wreaking havoc in My Sanctuary ♡ I, Yahweh, am known to defend the simple and My Heart melts for the pure of heart; he who comes to Me as a little child will know and will be allowed to meet with Wisdom ♡ who will lead him into My Kingdom; My Eyes

12

favour the little hearts, for in these hearts My Knowledge is poured in abundance; woe to those who do not welcome Me in simplicity of heart but show themselves as the greatest in My Courts and "call evil good, and good evil, who substitute darkness for light and light for darkness, who substitute bitter for sweet and sweet for bitter" ♡ (Is.5:2 My Spirit, seeing their selfish intentions, will divorce them from Me, who am thrice Holy; you want to enjoy Heaven? you want to rejoice in My Presence? then come to Me as a child! you want to meet Me and see Me? then come to Me with innocence in your heart; come to Me with a pure heart and the scales covering your eyes will fall so that you see My Glory and Me who was, is, and is to come; do not be ensnared into your pride for I will allow those little ones to trip you over; I, God am with you, daughter, be blessed thrice in Our Trinitarian Holiness

9. 1. 96

My house is in the Courts of Yahweh
and my spirit rejoices in the brilliance
of His Majesty thrice holy.
It is in You that my soul moves,
fulfills and goes on trusting.
It is in You Eternal Father
that my spirit languishes, desires
and seeks the Truth.

Deprive me not, O Celestial Father
from the Seven Gifts of Your Spirit,
but send them to me,
to light my way and
illumine my spirit,
bathing me in Your Divine Trinitarian
Holiness.

* My peace I give to you; if the ground refuses
to yield its fruit and the country has
turned into a desert, it is because of its

* The Creator speaks

apostasy .... My Holy Spirit is hardly remembered, proclaimed or relied on, this is why the earth has declined and your soul, like a dying star that lost its brilliance, has darkened; with the Law of the Triune God, Vassula, in your hearts, you can all say: "my God will hear me;" and I will grant you from the bottom of My Heart, the seven gifts of My Spirit if you ask Me; now, My Vassula, tell Me, do you think you have obtained your knowledge of My Kingdom on your own?

16

No; no my God, I knew nothing of Your Kingdom from the beginning.

do you think your prophecies came out of yourself, My child?

No, because Scriptures say: "No prophecies can come out of oneself."

blessed are you, for allowing My Holy Spirit to rest upon you and act in you; these are the things now I want to reveal, so that everyone on this earth can be drawn towards Me and live in My utter fullness and that every living creature can possess Me as I too would wish to possess them ♡

freedom is to be found in My Spirit, thrice Holy ♡ consolation and refreshment is to be found in My Spirit; your sinful passions can be washed away by My Spirit thrice Holy and He can offer you the freedom to serve Me in a new and delightful way, attracting hordes of nations into sanctity, because you would be renewed by My Holy Spirit; delightful child, write:

determined to share My Glory with all of you, I am ever so lavishly pouring out in your days, My Holy Spirit to renew you

18

so that you obtain your freedom in My Spirit, men are seeking their own ruin, but My Love is faithful and My Compassion is great.; I looked down at My creation and said: I will let the wind carry My Breath * to them sooner than I had planned; I will neither keep the scores nor the records; as My Ways are above your ways; My Breath will be carried by the winds on My creation, so that they say: "God has

* The Holy Spirit. – The Holy Spirit is already being poured out, e.g. charismatic movements.

19

not forgotten us, this is His dew, this is His raindrops;" and to accompany these I shall pour on you Instruction like prophecy, even to the least of you, creation, I shall pour out My Gifts so that you may see your nakedness and realize how, during all your lifetime you had grieved Me ♡ then, like a child, you will weep and turn to Me, your Father; from thereon you will aspire only after heavenly things that last; do not look for freedom elsewhere except in My Spirit; and like in the time of the first-fruits,* I will fill

*I heard at the same time the word: Apostles

20

you with a variety of gifts from My Holy Spirit; many of you will be singing in tongues, others will have the eloquence of speech; My gifts are numerous, and they will be given lavishly; come! come and win the friendship of My Holy Spirit to become collaborators with Him, for He will graciously initiate you into Our mysteries by opening your mind and your eyes to understand and perceive the Imperceptible yet graciously offered to you at no cost; Oh, come! do not stand there, inert,

21

come and inherit what is yours from the beginning; come and inherit the Inaccessible Light yet all around you and who could be within you! come and possess the Unattainable yet at everyone's reach! come! and do not stand remote and in terror, come and inherit the mystery of My Kingdom; today I am offering you Joy, Peace, your Inheritance I am offering you an Inestimable Treasure more beautiful than any man could conceive of obtaining; if I am pursuing you untiringly it is because of the greatness of the love I have for you, out of the favours I have favoured you this One is My Crown;* come closer to Me and I will breathe in you Immortality, reanimating your soul to move, aspire, and breathe in My Glory so that you no longer belong to yourself but to the One who moves you in union in Our Oneness; do not say: "do I dare, I, the sinner, apply for the Inaccessible Light? accessible only to the saints?" — if you <u>truly</u> believe you are a sinner, as you say,

* God is speaking of His Holy Spirit.

and unworthy for My Gifts, the impossible will become possible;* I will immediately set you on fire to consume you and burn to the root all that was not Me; I will then replace all that hindered My passage in you by the One whom you thought Unattainable; He will be the light of your eyes, the motive of your being, the movement of your heart, the utterance of your speech, your laughter and your joy, the kingly adornment

* God means that if we admit we are sinners, we already acknowledge our unworthiness; with a spirit of humility we can obtain His Spirit's Gifts.

24

of your soul, the watchman of your spirit; He will be your brother, your sister and your faithful friend; He will be your festivity, your banquet, the hidden treasure, the pearl, your hymn to the Hymn, your amen to the Amen; the promised land and the foundation of all virtues on which He will inscribe His Holy Name; come then and receive the Seal of your freedom by admitting you are a sinner and subject to sin, so that I, in My turn, lavish upon you My Inexhaustible Riches and the Kingdom of Heaven; My Holy Spirit can quench your thirst; I want to turn you all into a blameless race, into a holy people, into Our Image, so why, why do you ask from Me so very little.... and with so little faith? why do you misjudge My generosity? your lack of faith is a fatal poison for your spirit drawing you into what I repel: human doctrines and regulations; you have learnt that the Church is My Son's Body and that He is Its Head;*

* Col 1:18

this is why you, who make part of His Body, should aspire for the gifts of My Holy Spirit and penetrate into the mystery of Christ, mystery which will divinize you; in the power of My Spirit you will see a glorious vision of your inheritance where all the holy people rest, you will see your place of rest; - are you fit for My Kingdom? on whom do you rely? set your eyes, your mind and your heart on Me and come to possess My Kingdom; come and possess Me, your God; rely on no one else but Me; – the interior power within you is My Holy Spirit in whom you breathe and move, never ceasing to be; the interior charm, grandeur, eloquence and beauty within you is My Holy Spirit; the interior light of your soul is My Spirit thrice Holy that renders your soul imperishable, full of grace, My heaven, My rest and the perfect dwelling for Me, your God, triune but One in the unity of essence ♡ the interior Intercessor within you who lifts your spirit in a cloud and

brings you in communion with My Saints and My Angels is My Holy Spirit; He will teach you to be unshakeable when persecuted and calumniated for My sake; set your heart on perfecting your soul, filling it with My Spirit and you shall live!
– come, daughter, we, us? – God-is-with-you;

27. 1. 96

Yahweh, Father, You spoke to me as an Abba, as a Friend, I bless Your Name thrice Holy.

Your tenderness, embracing me, revealed the Path of Life to me and since then You built Your Palace and Your Dominion inside my soul.

Yes, as tenderly as a father treats his children, You treated me. Like someone handling a fine porcelain with care, You handled me.

You rose from Your Celestial Throne. You rose and stepped out, approaching me gently in Your Kingly air and while You posed Your Finger on my lips, You winked at me, producing a spring of joy in my heart!

Yahweh, my King, descended in my room; clothed in fearful splendour, in majesty and glory, my Creator and King spoke to me in simplicity, leaving me utterly bewildered, speechless and in awe because of His Paternal attitude.

30

You see? Yahweh You are the Joy and the ravishment of my soul; the delight of every hour of my day, the Consolation, the Goodness of my heart.

Your Love, Yahweh, is like a Spring, cascading over the mountains and into the valleys, giving life even to the stones!

Holy One, take me, take me and hide me in Your Pillar of cloud, away from the depths of this earth. Hide me in Your cloud from disorder, and as David once said, I too say: "Without Yahweh's help, I should, long ago, have gone to the Home of Silence." (Ps 94:17)

Holy One, great are Your achievements in my daily life, so come, O come Father, can't You see how my soul is craving for You? Come and leave me, once again, spellbound.

31

you are the fruit of My Wealth ....
delightful child, what is for Me to come into your room from the heavens? what is for Me to step down from My Throne and visit you? see? and what is for Me, My child, to fragrance you with My perfume? altogether it is nothing for Me; you heard Me knocking and you opened your door to Me; to converse with you delights Me; to visit you, sealing you every time with My Name, glorifies Me; to fragrance you with My Perfume establishes My Kingdom in

32

you; ah, Vassula, My company to you ravishes your soul, because all the words I whisper in your ear are life; accept My company and be ever at joy in My Presence, delighting to be with your Creator and Father of all; Wisdom is for children, so come to Me as a child, even at play* in My Presence; are you afraid My Words will scandalize?

I am sure they will for some!

* When God winks His Eye at me, He is being 'playful'.

every man judges from the store of his heart; all My Words I say are right and will be heard straightforward to him who understands, delightful to the simple and to the pure of heart, but to the jackals a scandal and an offence; never give the devil a foothold by your rationalistic spirit; grow not on illusions, but let your foundation grow in My Spirit; build your edifice in My Holy Spirit in whom you will be renewed. come and learn: however invisible I might appear,

34

I am to be found all around you and in things I have made. he who lives for Me will live with Me; he who loves his neighbour has already overcome the world and is well in the same footprints of My Son, Jesus Christ, and on his way to My Kingdom yes, anyone who lives in love lives a True Life in Me; I am your Father before your earthly father; I have fathered* you before your father of flesh; bind yourself to Me so that you do

* The Creator decides to create.

not lose Me from your sight and dishonour yourself; obey My principles but with a heart and not a rock; resolve to do right for the rest of your life but with a taste of joy; resolve to put an end to stifling My Holy Spirit of Grace around you so that you, too, can draw your breath in Him ♡ man! born of woman, honour The Woman adorned with the sun! feeble man! find your comfort in Her embrace and in those same arms that carried My Son through the desert into

Egypt; honour the Mother who honoured Me with Her graciousness, why, have I not highly favoured Her? I have done great things for the Woman clothed with the sun, so that from that day forward when My Spirit covered Her, all generations would call Her Blessed ♡

shame and dishonour are the lot who stopped honouring Her; I take no pleasure in your comments combined with sneers on the Woman so highly favoured by Me and to each I will pay his due;

37

humble your spirit, humble it even more now and abstain from making faces when it comes to entreat Her intercession; who tells you that I shall not listen to Her? Has your Mother not interceded in Cana? these signs were performed so that your spirit may understand what your spirit rejects today!* this sign was meant for all ages to come; the Woman adorned with the sun, adorned with My Holy Spirit, thrice

* God is speaking only to those who reject our Blessed Mother and to those who do not give Her enough honour.

38

Holy and who fills the world, ranks as Mother of God; come, My daughter, do your best and I shall do the rest; Yahweh in His glory blesses you, let your fruits increase ♡ *[1] flame of My Son's Eyes, remember you are not alone, I am with you ♡

30. 1. 96

My Spouse,*[2] do not let me return to You empty handed, let me come back to You with vessels of incense and vessels of fruits: a whole army ready to sacrifice themselves for Your Will.

*[1] This was uttered like a command.
*[2] Is 54: 5 "... Your Creator will be your husband..."

My sacrifice, live for Me, take your oil from Me; listen, break into joyful cries, should anyone attack you, for My sake, count this as an honour; feeble, oh feeble soul, when will you learn? when? why can I not feed you this daily bread of which I have tasted with fervour to save you and glorify My Father? you should ask for more, you should ask that it comes like rain on you; you say: "My Spouse, do not let Me return to you empty handed," and I tell you:

40

My Bride, how right you are, therefore, take the advice from your Spouse: plead for more sufferings, bring to Me this incense you have promised Me; recover, and come back to your senses; I could, if you let Me, overwhelm you with trials, set-backs, the lot; can you not see how highly favoured you are? do not brood anymore; remain the brilliant flame of My Eyes, and do not try to put it out....
indeed, I have you exposed as a banner with My insignia on you, to the world,

41

but the world refuses to see that the insignia is Mine so they pick up stones to hurl on My banner .... others pursue you like frenzied hunters, find your happiness in the tyranny they inflict on you, I will not allow them to give you more than what is necessary, the Almighty who is all-seeing will note every one of your steps; and if they wrong-do you more than your portion, My Father and I will relieve you, bringing you into your inheritance ♡ do not think that I Myself am not pierced when they pierce you, what they do to you they do to Me; I sigh with pain within you; they are tyrannizing Me in you; it costs Me no effort to remove a tyrant... but I tell you now, let it be so for a while and trust Me; I am sanctifying My dwelling place ♡ with a sacrifice ....

and now remain obedient to Me by keeping your vows of fidelity ....

they refused My gift of delight ....

they shed innocent blood and their hands are covered with this blood ♡ ic

31.1.96

My Beloved went down to my room to press me to His Sacred Heart and carry me away with Him, riding the winds. I am my Beloved's and my Beloved is mine forever.

Today my Beloved has the most sorrowful Eyes and His Head leans on my shoulder. 'Fountain of Living Water', who has grieved You so much?

My own have, My very own .... I am so worn out, there is no fathom to My sorrow... I cannot conceal My distress from you, Vassula.... nothing can be hidden between the two of us any more since I have set you so close to Me;

44

hear what your Beloved has to say now: He who created you, your Maker and your Divine Father has decided to lift your soul to Him ..... I am making no secret of this, yes! My Father stood up, His cry echoing in every heavenly ear; He stood up, He who fostered you, father-like and who guided you, offering you as His gift to humanity, to take you back to Him; being God He does not fail to see your innocence; being God, He does not see as mankind sees and I tell you, He has risen*, for the

* "Risen," is for "stood up."

45

tyranny they inflict on you has outweighed every measure put together .... My question to you is: "do _you_ want your Father who is in Heaven to snatch you from the tyrants' hands and from falsehood's lips?

Lord, have I not made a pact with You? I made a pact with my eyes, not to see for the first three days of my life. I had made a pact with my Creator and my Beloved to remain in the dark and forbid my eyes to see the sun in its glory and the glow of the moon streaking on me so that I may accomplish my mission till the end and glorify You.

46

My Vassula, to you I ask again: "do you want to prolong your suffering, My child, on earth, or do you want to wake up in the morning in My Light, in Our embrace surrounded by thousands of angelic voices where safety, glory and Sweetness Itself will surround you?

Ah, my God, my soul thirsts for You. My soul longs for You. I could simply say now: "Come! come and rescue me to enjoy Your closeness forever. My soul melts within me with love for You. My spirit can be succumbing into Your Hands any moment now and I could be, if I wished, on my way to the House of my God among cries of joy and praise and an exultant throng, I can be with the God of my Joy! But, I want to be an object of scorn among the dead and their pestilential tyranny of me. Fatherless I am not, You are with me; Scriptures say: "If a man is innocent, You, my Saviour, will bring him freedom." You have given my hand free play now, to choose.

Holy One, I want nothing for my own and then, it is You who endowed me with life, with joy, binding me to You. And, it is You who watched each breath of mine with tender care and so the Song You want to sing can continue to be sung for the freedom of many nations and You can continue playing on Your harp, my God, for the Beast will cower before You

48

in the end. Use me as an object of scorn and have me still where dimness and disorder hold sway and where light itself is like the dead of night.

but they are molesting you!

For the greatest of Your Glory! Let it be. Let them molest me.

My daughter, let it be then as you wish; I bless you in Our Trinitarian Holiness; but tell Me: what shall I do when My Father stands up again?

Remind Him of our pact, Lord.

at this My own Heart melts .... My remnant,

49

I will save many by your very wretchedness, by your generosity, but remember, every motion of yours that honours Me comes from Me.... so avoid any tendency to self-esteem .... be patient for a little while longer; have I ever seen a wretch in need of love, without giving him My Heart? see, I am your Friend; no one can say: "the Lord imposes His orders on us...." and to you, daughter, I say: "I am glad you have not broken your pact with My Father; I shall use your generosity to bless every

50

man on earth and pour out My Mercy before the day of disaster; I will pour out a spirit of kindness and prayer; I tell you, I, the Lord, will turn you into a Fortress, I shall build you strong with My power; ah .... My Heart rejoices in you! let our eyes meet and feast in this joy! I will bring many back to Me, those that have been led astray will finally return to Me .... come, lean on the God of your Joy! never lose heart, remember, I too, when I was condemned and given My Cross to carry, I fell on the same ground that bears you all, but I was lifted up to complete My Work; learn then from your Saviour; in the end the gain will be yours .... the breath of Omnipotence will lift you up again; from your ordeals I shall draw life*[1] in abundance; know this: your Father will answer you from His Holy Place; at your side I Am! ....

My Father ....

I Am;*[2] today I will give you to the

*[1] Conversions
*[2] The Eternal Father speaks

52

nations and I will be your encircling Shield. today you have crowned Me with glory; tyranny and injustice are surrounding innocent blood and My Heart was ready to lift you from Tyranny, how could I remain silent when I watch your oppressors lurking to ambush you and your counsellor? how could I remain silent when what I hear is: "how shall we track them down?" but here is the consolation I am offering you*[1]: seek to do good, maintain*[2]

*[1] To all of us *[2] It sounded like: 'Keep up.'

justice, I am with you .... remain faithful, the times are so evil; I do not want to say one day: "look, there is My daughter, she lies all alone on her soil, with no one to lift her up;" I filled your*[1] nostrils with My Strength, and I lit a flame inside you to maintain justice .... all that you do, do so in a spirit of gentleness,*[2] even if your testimony is not accepted, be in peace; do not look to your left nor to your right;

*[1] Fr. O'Carroll.
*[2] I heard simultaneously 'firmness' too.

54

many will rise declaring they are sent by Me;* do not be sold to them again .... do not be afraid, you will not be put to shame; — and to you, My daughter, I will comfort you and all those who trust Me; the times are evil, but, remember, your Creator leans tenderly over you all; work with peace in My Name; adorn My Name with your love and continue to plant vineyards in arid lands; I am your Father, let Me be your consolation,

* False prophets

55

remembering that My Love for you will never leave you; – and you* who say: "I protest against such injustice, there is no reply, if I appeal against it, judgment is never given; they have stolen my honour away...." I tell you: if they denied you what your pen entreated, be in peace.... what more honour could they have given you? in the end, My friend, will I not see that justice be given? I am Lord and My blessing is yours; ✝

* Fr. O' Carroll

56

know you valiant in battle;* but leave this honour to Me; continue to plant in My House .... I will see that you will continue to remain fresh so that you bear fruit in spite of your old age ♡ daughter, your consent out of your love for Me touched Me to tears ....! happy are you who are poor; yours is My Kingdom ♡ I am King in you ..... through this weakness I shall break

* I sensed God's humour and my heart leaped with joy!

57

the power of the wicked;*[1] I bless you, My child ♡

Rhodos 12. 2. 96

My Lord?

I Am; learn, My Vassula, from the saints; I am not a complicated God, I am not far either; I do not hide My Face nor do I keep anyone in the dark; My mere Presence is Light! many of you say:*[2] "Lord bring

*[1] 'My Power is at its best in weakness' 2 Co. 12:9
*[2] This message was given 5 min. before a telephone call for an interview on Radio Dublin. The interviewer ended by asking: "Is Jesus saying something new to us?"

58

us something new..." this is the spirit of Antichrist and this spirit is at large in the world; I will bring you nothing new; I have died, I have risen, I am the First and the Last, he who believes in Me will have everlasting life; I am alive forever and in glory, and I hold the keys of death and of Hades; there are still things to come, but everything has been written until the end of Times ♡ I will come to restore your sight with My Spirit to accomplish what I have said....

59

that in the end I shall triumph; today still My land is being divided, riven, and in My House and My household there is selling and buying; to the prophets I am sending them, they say: 'do not prophesy'; that time I was telling you previously has come, when Cardinal will go against Cardinal, bishop against bishop; priest against priest; the Divider's power has infiltrated like smoke into My House to besiege My land; his destructive work is strong and his favourite targets are

60

My consecrated souls; he turns their thoughts to follow the passions of their hearts; the Rebel, wherever he passes leaves his curse behind .... he has sworn to lift you one against another; he has sworn, in his fury, to sift you all especially My consecrated ones and plunder them; he has sworn to use you all as his toy; I tell you: anyone whose heart is not upright will succumb, but the upright will live through faithfulness; be strong Vassula; I,

61

Jesus, bless you and your comrades; - do not judge; we, us? I love you; - peace - ic

20.2.96

Please Lord, look at this branch of Yours; Visit it and check on it. It has been shaken; has the Vine felt how it was tormented?

yes, since the branch belongs to Me, the true Vine; My branch, do not worry as long as you are part of the true Vine and bear fruit; My Love heals; count on Me and on no one else;

62

pray more and ask for more from Me; why do you shy away from Me? come to Me, child, and you will obtain; I love you .... allow My Finger on your lips so that from these will echo My Words; accept all that comes from Me; rest in Me and allow Me to rest in you; I am Lord, I am the Alpha and the Omega so deepen your faith in Me; dearest child, love one another and never fail Me; My Love is in your heart to console you; come; ic

63

18. 3. 96

peace be with you; My Command to you is:* go out where I send you to bear fruit that will last ♡ the Amen is with you; go round offering all that you have learnt from Me; by the power of My Holy Spirit you shall walk, you shall talk, you shall move hearts, you shall cast out devils, you shall uproot evil and you shall plant goodness; and I, will rejoice at My choice; rejoice, too, in your

* God had a very powerful and commanding Voice.

64

God; even after your death, your body will still keep prophesying; – you see My Spirit will express Himself through your body; I, and I only, preached to you: 'Salvation'; My Power is at its best in weakness, I have found Weakness and I have become your real Friend; you want now to be pleasing to Me?

Yes, my God and Father.

work faithfully in My Name, thrice Holy and carry out My Command in union with the one* I have united you with and

* Fr. O'Carroll

Excerpts from Notebook 83

19 March 96, NB p.1...I am losing so many...every day!

✠ Do not fail the starved waiting out there; do not shrink from visiting the sick

✠ See this seed? ...once sown will give you the bread of suffering, it will also be to your profit...I shall honour you with My Thorned Crown

✠ With little time left now, do not delay, for I am afflicted beyond your understanding

20-26 March 96 (The Annunciation, 25 March), NB p.9...Let the whole world bend their knee to Her who bears the Sacred Name: Mother of God

✠ Let all who live on earth revere Her Immaculate Heart

✠ The islands, the mountains, the hills, the valleys and the springs all bow low when She passes by them

✠ You who stand in Our Presence stand ever so close to all who invoke You

✠ How has man fallen so low and taken a deceptive path to deny Your Heart?

✠ Have you not noticed how My Heart melts and favours always Her Heart

✠ Lift your eyes, creation, at the sight of Her Heart and I promise you, you will never stop growing in radiance

✠ Before the floods of sin overtake you! Come in this Ark that can save you

✠ If you acknowledge Her Heart, not only will you be acknowledging My Heart but also the Father's

✠ All the moments My Holy Mother spent on earth were a perfect hymn of Love, charity, humility and purity

✠ My words and My thoughts did not need to be carried to Her in My absence

✠ My Angels tremble for that day I will pronounce these people guilty!

✠ That day I was conceived by the Holy Spirit in Her virginal Womb, all the demons were paralysed with fright

- ✠ Let your life become an ornament of beauty, a wreath of flowers, an increasing smoke of incense
- ✠ Let no one deceive you by telling you that God has no means of approaching His people...do not allow these people to disturb your spirit

3 April 96, NB p.44...What had been lost and profaned by Eve was to be gained and sanctified by the Virgin Mary

- ✠ Apostles of the end times...would be instructed by the Queen of Heaven and Myself
- ✠ They would pursue them with My Cross in one hand, and the rosary in the other
- ✠ This enmity is not only given between the Queen of Heaven and Satan, but...between Her children whose empire is in Her Heart, and the children of the Devil who have built their kingdoms in him and through him
- ✠ She is the Joy of My Sacred Heart, The Joy of My celestial court
- ✠ Run to your Blessed Mother, who...will hide you too under Her Mantle
- ✠ Your time of lust is almost over now
- ✠ Turn to the Virgin of virgins and become another little Jacob
- ✠ In these end of times, the Queen of Peace is passing over the earth, escorted by My Angels
- ✠ I have given...all the jewels of Wisdom in Her Heart and from this treasury She gives abundantly Her graces to take you out of the power of darkness

healed and let him put up more generously with the faults of the weak whom I have raised and blessed; stand your ground for this work of Mercy; resist evil and cling to Me; go, and do not be afraid to declare the truth; My Holy Spirit will remove all bounds to the truth; My Name: Peace and Love;

A ☧ Ω

19. 3. 96

Vassula-of-My-Sacred Heart: the Viper, it is the Viper that brings death that

2

is crawling around you all; he tempts, he waits, he waits for your fall; then death does not delay to come; ah .... My Sacred Heart is in pain ....

Lord, I am here, what can I do for You to relieve Your pain?

follow My Command*[1] to the letter! death must not come; can you see what I see every day? no .... no you cannot see what I see .... I am losing thousands of lives,*[2] I am losing so many ... every day!

*[1] Message of 18.3.96
*[2] Jesus was crying very hard and was in agony

3

have *you* seen what I have seen out there in the desert? there are thousands who are starving and are thirsty for consolation, hope and love; there are thousands who are naked and in need of My words; My compassion extends to everything that lives! but, look! the Tempter wants to beggar you so that you *will* have nothing to offer; come, stretch your hand out to the needy; do not fail the starved waiting out there; do not shrink from visiting the sick;

— Vassula, I had resolved to have you

4

as My bride so that you follow Me; I made you My bride and I have placed My Lamp* inside you, so that in the Light of My Holy Spirit and through His Power you would start reasoning not as mortals reason, but as My angels in heaven are reasoning; I, then, fortified you with My Spirit of Fortitude to withstand the heavy blows of the enemy and to stand your ground; I have given you My Spirit of Counsel to show you what delights Me

* Jesus means the Holy Spirit.

5

most; I have opened the gates to heaven and shown you My saints* who journeyed through poverty, but fed and covered the naked, who journeyed through humility and obedience leaving space for My Spirit to act in them and produce through their loyalty prodigies; they have journeyed through mortification, spittle and suffering, but rejoiced all the more for this honour and asked for more while offering everything to Me; — creature! you have still a long

* Vision of: 27. 9. 87

6

way to go, but the prize will be yours too if you accept ardently all that I am offering you; My bride, do not fear, if in every course you take, you have Me in your mind: look, in one Hand I have a seed that once sown it will grow, giving you contentment for all that you will be able to achieve for Me, never wearying; and it will adorn your neck because honours will be worn around your neck like an ornament of beauty; and your head will be covered by

7

perfumes dripping like dew from your hair; now, look in My other Hand ... see this seed ? this, once sown, will give you the bread of suffering, it will also be to your profit*; there will be wounds and wounds again, and again, and I will raise your closest friends to turn into your biggest persecutors, you will stifle and moan; I shall honour you with My Thorned Crown, My Nails and My Cross!; I will, My friend, offer you to drink daily from My Cup until the bitterness of

* Profit = sanctification

8

My Cup will not give you a moment to draw breath; now, come and choose one of the seeds; if you choose the first one, you will have your suffering later on; - choose!

I want Your Will, You are God and You choose for me

very well then, My bride, I will choose the second seed; you will be persecuted, but never by your closest friends, I will not allow it, ah how I rejoice, for you have behaved as I would have you behave, leaving everything in My Hands and remaining a Nothing; - are you finally realizing that I suffice

9

by Myself? I do not intend to hide My Inexhaustible Riches in these times of need but I will cast them out through your nothingness; with little time left now, do not delay, for I am afflicted beyond your understanding; hurry, for death is imminent out there in the desert; delight in Delight; I bless you; IC

(Received from:
– The Announciation: 25.3.96 – (20 – 26) 3.96

I am your servant and I am here to serve You, Majesty, without You I am nothing, Pure Contentment of my soul, I am listening.

My beloved, come and learn: who has

10

exalted Me most? I will tell you who exalted Me most: the New Eve has; yes! the Woman adorned with the sun, standing on the moon, and with the twelve stars on Her Head for a crown;*[1] for I who made heaven and all that is in it, and earth and all it bears and the sea and all it holds*[2] have placed Her above all these things;*[3] the Queen of heaven

*[1] Ap. 12:1
*[2] Ap. 10:6
*[3] The sign of this is that She stands on the moon.

11

is always in the presence of the Most High's throne; no less than the height of heaven over earth is the greatness of Her Name, Her Name, wrapped in a robe of light; let the whole world bend their knee to Her who bears the Sacred Name:

Mother of God;

in Her Immaculate womb She glorified Me by receiving Me, the unblemished Lamb, making a sanctuary for the Sanctuary, come and sing a new song in Her honour, let all who live on earth revere Her;

12

Immaculate Heart, the Altar, in which I was conceived and became God-Man too,* no one glorified Me as much as the Woman adorned with the sun; yes! She is so superbly beautiful in Her perfect Love that the islands, the mountains, the hills, the valleys and the springs all bow low when She passes by them; and today as yesterday, when Most Fair Love passes over the earth, escorted by My Angels whose eyes never

* Jesus adds too because He is God as well.

13

cease admiring the Admirable, Holiest of all Virgins, marvelling at the Beauty of My Father's Masterpiece, when She passes over the earth, She lovingly intervenes, and answers your entreaties; let Me tell you: My Sacred Heart is your heaven; creation, My Sacred Heart, that so many of you deny and refuse, is your Heaven, your Paradise, your Kingdom; your Inheritance, your Place-of-Rest for Eternity; so approach this Heart that loves you so and I will pour out, from My Heart,

14

in your heart countless blessings, to turn your soul as fair as springtime, to turn your soul into an ivory tower, a heaven for Myself alone; how can anyone doubt of My Love? ah, beloved, every time you doubt of My Love, the sun darkens in My distress ... ! today, I want to display in My great Love, the Heart of My Mother,

[2] "O Masterpiece of My Father!
O Sublime Masterpiece of Yahweh!

---

[1] I felt Jesus' Heart melting with love when pronouncing the word "Mother".

[2] With a loud cry Jesus was speaking to our Lady

15

Spouse to My Holy Spirit! My Radiant Tabernacle! Your Heart, Beloved of the Beloved*[1], is One with Ours! Your Heart is My enclosed garden, a sealed fountain; your Heart is a Fountain that makes the gardens fertile; your Heart, Adorable One, is My Throne, on which I have been honoured; Heart of the Heart, whom I crowned in Our presence and in the presence of all My celestial court,*[2] how can any of My creatures

[1] I understood 'Beloved' as for the Beloved Trinity.
[2] Suddenly Christ lowered His Voice becoming sad.

16

deny Your Heart?[1] You, the Ark of power, all vested in virtues, My New Song,[2] My Harp, My Citadel, in whom the Maker of heaven and earth is ravished by Your magnificence, You who stand in Our Presence stand ever so close to all who invoke You; yet, how has man fallen so low and taken a deceptive path to deny Your Heart? have you not heard, creation, that I am the Heart of Her Heart? the Soul of Her

[1] Jesus at the same time was sad and amazed.
[2] I understood that it meant the New Eve.

17

Soul, the Spirit of Her Spirit? have you not heard that Our Two Hearts are united in One? consider My Redemptive Heart, consider Her Co-Redemptive Heart, consider the Delight of My Heart, rising like the dawn to brighten the earth in its darkness, consider the Queen's Heart that shines on mankind brighter in Her radiance than all the constellations put together, more resplendent than the sun; radiant as My Glory because of Her unique perfection!; consider the Tabernacle of your God; consider and

18

esteem highly as I esteem My Throne; do not ask: "how could it be that the Most High has assigned Her such a high throne in His Celestial Courts?" look, not only have I assigned Her as the Queen of My Angels and My creatures but I have assigned Her to be My Throne. the Queen of heaven and earth is the Throne of the King of kings, for I, the Lord of All, have placed Her as first in My Sacred Heart; born to be My Crown of Splendour, born to be the Vessel of the True Light who was made

19

flesh from David's line, born to be My honour and My boast, the Spirit with Me and the Father said: 'Mary full of grace, We are with you, We will hide none of the secrets from You, Our Breath will be your breath, pure emanation of Our Glory, Mary Our image of Our Goodness, We give you Our Peace in Your Heart, in this perfect Heart I, the Son shall triumph; Our Heart will be Your Heart, a burning furnace of divine love, Our Soul will be Your Soul*, an august treasure, a Paradise for Us, Our

*soul should be understood as life, as in Lk 9:24

20

Spirit will be Your Spirit; yes, for anyone who is joined to Us is one spirit with Us ♡ " this is the One whom We so highly favoured, the One whom so many reject and yet is the ointment of your eyes, the balm to your wounds, the merciful plead to the Eternal Father for your pleas; the intercessor and your advocate of your soul, feeble man ... the Spouse of My Holy Spirit is the Temple of the Temple!, the promised land of the weak and the wretched, the reflection of My eternal Light; the consoler of Your Consoler is the comfort of your sorrows .... what has man to say? what can man say in his tent? how can he discover anything celestial in his perishable body when his soul is weighed down by sin, what the all-powerful Hand of My Father has done? you govern your mind, man, with no light, no sense; today, man, open your heart, then, all the mysteries that appeared to you fathomless will be revealed to you by My Divine Light, thrice Holy, and you

22

will understand who the Woman adorned with the sun, is; then, your whole being will be lifted and your heart will be exulted and in rapture when your eyes will be unveiled to see the Blessed Heart of the blessed hearts, the Most Holy of saints, the Incomparable Heart, burning with unlimited love, a fire alight and so bright; then, My friend, you will understand what Virtue is, and how in this Virtuous Virginal Heart, I, God, became God-Man, you will see the Mother of your Saviour, Mother of the

23

prophets, Mother of the disciples, Mother of charisms, Mother of Triumph; Mother of unlimited graces; Mother of unequalled Redemption ♡ the Vineyard of the True Vine, the Path ♡ to the Path that leads everyone to Me, the Gate wide open to heaven for everyone to enter and have everlasting life; – have you not noticed how My Heart melts and favours always Her Heart? how can this Heart, who bore your King, be denied anything She asks from Me? all the faithful bless Her Heart for in

24

blessing Her Heart you will be blessing Me; Queenly and adorable you will proclaim Her once you get to know Her; so lift your eyes, creation, at the sight of Her Heart and I promise you, you will never stop growing in radiance; your heart will be lifted into the furnace of Her Heart, and, throbbing with delight and full, you will enter Her Heart as one entering an ocean of love, since the riches of Her Heart are as wide as the Sea that flows to you and you to this Sea; the Wealth of heaven and

25

earth lie all in Her Heart and they can be all for you! though night still covers your mind and heart, arise! arise and lift your eyes at this radiant sight of Her Heart, that so many prophets wanted to see in their time, but had not seen It; arise and sing a new hymn to the Hymn of the Most Holy Trinity, sing and say: "brothers! sisters! come and be covered by the Mantle of Grace in Grace; come and be covered by the Queen's Light; come, let us be overshadowed by the One

26

who was overshadowed by the Holy Spirit;" have you not heard how the nations will come to Her Light and that the kings will come to Her dawning brightness, when in the end Her Heart will triumph together with Mine? mystery for the rich in heart, but for the poor and the lowly a Blessing so longed for .... O come! before the floods of sin overtake you! come in this Ark* that can save you; do not be like your ancestors in the days of Noah, who did

* In our Blessed Mother's Heart.

27

not listen; come into the Ark and you will be saved from the tempestuous waters of sin, and from perishing in the floods of sin; come and become the promised child of the Mediatrix as a result of the devotion you would have had for Her; in your devotion for Her you will be devoting yourself to Me; every devotion, honouring Her Heart, will amplify and ascend on Me since Our union is so perfect; in your devotion for Her Heart, all My decrees will be better understood in Her Light, because your steps

28

will be guided by Her Heart since your hand will be taken by the Throne of Graces Herself; how blessed you will be to repeat your devotion to Her Heart! come to the One, so Blessed, who shows Her Motherly Love to Her children by showing them the way to heaven; come to the Co-Redemptrix of your Redeemer whose Heart, burning with Love, was offered to be pierced too for your sake; come and honour this Heart, alight as a Lamp, shining within and without near My Heart; if you say: "we have no use for Her Heart", know that in reality you are saying: "we have no use for the Lord's Heart!" learn, feeble man, that My Sacred Heart and the Immaculate Heart of your Mother are so united that in their perfect unity those Two Divine Hearts become One; I tell you solemnly: if you acknowledge Her Heart, not only will you be acknowledging My Heart but also the Father's; have I not said that I am in the Father and the Father is in Me? if I am in the Father and the Father is in Me, My Heart,

30

too, is in the Father and His Heart is in Mine, to say that We are not inseparable and One, is to deny My Word ♡ do not be the slave of your spirit and do not be won by the arguments of the world; tell Me, which creature's heart is like unto Mary's Heart? there is none like unto Mary's Heart, perfect from the beginning, Immaculate from birth* and full of Grace, surpassing in its grace My Angels' graces; this is why My Angels in throngs questioned one another: "who is this,

* she was conceived Immaculate

31

behind Her veil?" "why are the crests of the mountains bowing down low, saluting Her, as She passes them by?" "who is this without a blemish in Her Heart and so pleasing to God?" "have you seen how all God's creation lowers its gaze as She passes by?" "who is She who is like a fountain that makes the gardens fertile by Her graces, this well of living water?" "who is She, with a Heart so pure with divine love, aspiring for God day and night, night and day, and in

32

perfect union with the Most High?"
"who is this Virgin who is so humble over Her great wealth of virtues and graces, that the supreme God's Eyes never leave Her?" many of My Angels remained silent in admiration, words had failed them.... it is in that Heart, in that Abyss of grace, I exercised My power ♡ the Author of heaven and earth, the Author of grace found His heaven in heaven, His grace in grace, to come in the condition of a slave, I came to Prodigious Humility* to

* Our Blessed Mother

serve and not to be served. I, the Redeemer of all mankind, the promised Messiah, came to the perfect image of My Sacred Heart to share the sorrows, the joys, the sufferings, the martyrdom, the wonders, the betrayals, the agonies, the scourging, the piercing, and the crucifixion; together Our Hearts atoned; all the moments My Holy Mother spent on earth, were a perfect hymn of love, charity, humility and purity; a treasure from My treasures; I came in this Holy Heart, image and

34

likeness to My Sacred Heart, to become God-Man so that I follow Her steps[1] and that later on She follows Mine[2]. I have said that She and I shared everything all the way to the Cross; Our union was so intimately perfect that We did not need speech, for the sole utterance was in Our Heart; My words and My thoughts did not need to be carried to Her in My absence; in the supreme power of My Holy Spirit, everything

[1] When Jesus was a child following His Mother
[2] I understood that Mary followed Jesus in His Missi

was known to Her; in Her virginal Heart everything was known to Her, since She possessed God and God possessed Her; in this way Her daily nourishment was the Will of the Eternal Father; oh creation! My Soul is in utter dismay when so many of you deny Her Heart! and My Angels tremble for that day I will pronounce these people, guilty! but for those who honoured Her and loved Her, the Gate of Her Heart will be open for you to step into heaven; and I will say to you who love and honour Her: "come! your love for Her was so great on earth that today you may come to your room and before My Holy Temple*[1] bow down;" creation, this Great Sign*[2] in heaven, the Woman adorned with the Sun that holds the demons paralysed with fear, this Great Sign that illuminates the heavens terrifying the Darkness*[3] is none other than My Mother; in contrast to the darkness I raised this Most Holy Virgin to be for all of you a Pillar of blazing

*[1] Our Blessed Mother: The Temple of God
*[2] Ap. 12:1
*[3] The Devil

fire by night to guide your step, and by day a Sun to illuminate your dreadful gloom; – that day I was conceived by the Holy Spirit in Her virginal Womb, all the demons were paralysed with fright while in heaven at the same time a great throng of the heavenly host were praising God and singing: "Glory to God in the highest heaven, and peace to men who enjoy His favour;" thus, I descended from heaven to heaven, from My throne to My throne.... yes, where every virtue was blossoming

38

ravishing My Sacred Heart by the fragrance of Her perfect Love; My Perfect One's Heart is unrivalled and altogether lovable ... Her Heart, since Her Immaculate Conception was an incessant prayer, an atoning incense, an incessant adoration for God; this is My Vineyard* whom My Father's powerful Hand cultivated so that the True Vine puts His root in that soil; come to the Heart of your Blessed Mother, which is as bright as day, come and receive Her graces, which

* Our Lady

39

are so innumerable, and that flash in rays from Her Hands. My Heart, which is full of grace and truth was made flesh in the Virginal Womb full of grace and truth; and now, Our Two Hearts, joined in One, will conquer Bitter Plague, not by physical strength nor by force of arms, but by love and sacrifice ♡

20-26. 3. 96

My Peace I give to you; in this Peace receive My Message .... *

* I asked Jesus what will happen if 'someone' will not obey, or listen to His requests.

40

all he has to do is read My message, then, let him decide, ♡ daughter, <u>all creation</u> obeys Me!...

Yes, the creation obeys You, but Your creatures, not all of them obey You!

no.... not all of them obey Me; many of them are tempted, and want to win the approval of men rather than Mine.... many are more eager to please men before Me, their God, and for some, it is only self-interest that makes them disobey Me; others have not yet decided to

41

put behind them their passions, their self-indulgences, they sin as much as they breathe; I have talked about judging others and how their tongue will be the cause of their condemnation, yet, on this, I can add one more thing: the mouths that spit fire, by snapping on people, tearing them to pieces, these too will suffer since they grieve My Holy Spirit; My Holy Spirit's ways are <u>so</u> different! anyone led by My Spirit is given the grace to observe My Laws and My Ways

42

which are gentle, loving and so perfect; I am the Source of Love and Jesus is My Name; but the Evil one is the source of Evil and all wickedness .... daughter, never lose courage, let your life become an ornament of beauty, a wreath of flowers, an increasing smoke of incense, so that the Image of the unseen God becomes visible to you for all eternity; remain faithful to Me; I am by your side, never fear! praise Me, daughter; peace.... ΙΧΘΥΣ 

20-26.3.96

My Lord, my Life, my Family, I am part of You and my spirit exults in You. I bless Your Name for ever and ever. Celebrate, creation, God's acts of power, and praise Him who raises the lowly, how can any mortal doubt on Your marvellous interventions?

My Vassula, let your life be an incessant prayer to Me... let no one deceive you by telling you that God has no means of approaching His people... do not allow these people to disturb your spirit; incense of Mine, pray for these people so that they, too, come and drink from My Foun-

44

tain and be revived; if they are ill-disposed and are reluctant to hear and understand, it is because they have abandoned Me and My Laws; ah...* Vassula, My flower, this generation has become a land of drought; pray for the conversion of the world ♡ IC

3. 4. 96

My Vassula, My little pupil of these end of times, I will dictate to you now a heavenly discourse on My Mother's Heart... as I have said to you previously,

* A sigh

45

My Mother's Heart and Mine are so united that They become One; the Virgin of virgins, the Holiest, forever now in Heaven, My Mother, continues to be proclaimed in Heaven as: My Mother*; when I, God, descended to be conceived by the Holy Spirit and be born of the Virgin Mary, I came into My heaven! I descended from one heaven into the other, I left one throne to sit on the other, like the lamp shining on the sacred lamp-stand, I found Her Heart,

* Title of: 'Mother of God' 'Theotokos'

46

shining from within and without ♡ I have been welcomed in this Paradise to be glorified; what had been lost*¹ and profaned by Eve was to be gained*² and sanctified by the Virgin Mary through Her perfect obedience and humility; and through this Woman, My Reign on earth will once more come; My Reign on earth will be founded in each heart; once more there

*¹ Eve lost the entry to Paradise for Herself and all her children.

*² Mary gained the entry to Paradise and for all Her children by the Redemption and Sacrifice of Jesus.

47

will be poured on you My Spirit, so lavishly, that this aridity of now will be transformed into a fertile land; it had been said that at the end of times, Our Two Hearts would raise apostles, and they would be called: apostles of the end of times; these would be instructed by the Queen of Heaven and by Myself, to go forward in every nation, to proclaim without fear the Word of God, even when they would be drenched with blood, by the Enemy's vicious attacks, they shall not be broken, their tongue

48

would pierce the enemies of My Church, like a double-edged sword, by exposing their heresies; they would never stagger, nor would they know fear, because I would provide them with a spirit of courage; the destructive whip would not catch them; they would not leave one stone unturned, they would pursue the sinners, the lofty speakers, the great and the proud, the hypocrites, the traitors of My Church, they would pursue them with My Cross in one hand, and the rosary in the other;

49

<u>and We would stand by their side</u>; they would shatter the heresies and build faithfulness and truth in their place; they would be the antidote of the poison, because they would sprout, like buds, from the Royal Heart of Mary*; these apostles of the end of times would call on God their Father, and God their Father, would call on their spirit; they would call on Mary, their Blessed Mother, and their Blessed Mother would call on them to become witnesses of the Most High ♡ and

* Jesus means that Mary will form them.

50

the Holy Spirit would give them a spirit of zeal to be ready for God, to be ready for this Battle; that day, the haughty crown of the powers of evil will be trampled underfoot by the Woman adorned with the sun, and by all Her children; the second Eve, in whom I have given enough power to overthrow Satan and his empire, will crush his head with Her heel this enmity is not only given between the Queen of heaven and Satan, but it is given as well between Her children

51

whose empire is in Her Heart, and the children of the Devil, who have built their kingdoms in him and through him, and who are in your days your biggest persecutors; many of these are worshippers of the Beast, the scholars and the philosophers of your times ... I, in My Trinitarian holiness, had chosen this humble Maiden to become in Her perfect virtues and graces, the Woman who would challenge, by Her virtues and graces, the entire kingdom of Lucifer, who constantly flies into a rage and who trembles with fear at the sound of Her Name; I tell you, no less than the height of heaven over the earth is the greatness, the power and the splendour of Her Name; let all who live on earth revere before the Queen's Heart; She has never ceased protecting Her children from the ambushes of the Evil one, who, in your times, has* set out openly to give battle to My Sacred Heart, and to all the army of My saints; but soon,

* the Evil one.

53

the empire of the Evil one will be broken up and his sovereignty will be uprooted by the powerful Hand of Mary;* in all truth I tell you: there is no one on earth or in heaven, or in the angelic powers that has been given such great authority and power over all, as your Blessed Mother, after My Power and My Authority; for I am the Alpha and the Omega, the First and the Last, the One who is, who was, and who is to come; I suffice by Myself as you know, but it

* Fatima's message: "In the end My Heart will triumph.

54

is through Mary's Virginal Heart, that My Redemptive plan began and it will be again through this Holy Heart that I will accomplish My Salvation plan; so honour Her Heart, you who fly into a rage at the sound of Her Name and understand that She is the Joy of My Sacred Heart, the Joy of My celestial court; Her thoughts from the day of Her Conception were always in union with My thoughts, Her Heart, in total submission to My Father's Will, was an

55

incessant prayer, an incessant hymn of love, an adoration to Me, your triune God, but One in the unity of essence – today, in these end of times, where the battle is raging on Our Two Hearts,* and on Our children who witness the Truth, I tell you: run to your Blessed Mother, who, like a hen who hides her chicks under her wings, will hide you, too, under Her Mantle; ah... but so many of you have perished even before you were born, with all the prohibitions to the devotions

* Allusion to Ap. 11 'The Two Witnesses

56

you once had on Her Virginal Heart! all because of your human doctrines and your rationalistic regulations, you have regulated your heart and your life according to this worldly life; O slaves of Sin! Slaves of money! Slaves of Satan! consider yourselves dead and putrefied! well then, your time of lust is almost over now; have you not heard that the Splendour of Dawn* is going to reign and shine in each

* Jesus means His Reign to come

57

heart that has been consecrated to Our Two Divine Hearts from which they will obtain divinization? that divinization that the human race lost at its fall .... since sin entered the world through one man, and through sin death, yet My plan of Redemption was to be laid out by Mary's Co-Redemptive Heart, the second Eve, perfected in the Image of God, so that I, the New Adam, would find My Paradise in Her Immaculate Heart; will I hear from you, generation: "my heart is ready, Lord, to learn to love and honour the Tabernacle that carried Your Sacred Heart; it is true, that from the womb I have gone astray, I have been in error since my birth; like Esau I have been running away from my Mother to look after my interests and achieve them by harrying others, I have been depending on my own strength; I hated my brother who, contrary to my heart, meditated on how to please our Mother's Heart and remained near Her,

59

receiving in abundance Her Graces; I have not been like Jacob and his descendants, Lord, my heart is ready to learn and love with honour the Sanctuary of the Sanctuary Most Holy, so that no deceit will enter any more in my spirit ever so spiteful, who harassed, like Cain, his brother then finally killed him; I will stop hounding those who belong to Her Immaculate Heart, but instead turn to the Virgin of virgins and become another little Jacob, so that in

60

Her Graciousness, She pours out of Her Virginal and Immaculate Heart, on me, abundant graces so that my soul, once Hers will feast on Her riches, making my heart an ornament of beauty in the Ornament of Beauty; let my heart, Lord, desire and long to gaze on Your Sanctuary* to see Your Power and Authority, to gaze in the Treasury of the Sanctuary and feast most richly; do not allow my soul,

* Mary's Heart.

61

any more, Lord, to go down to the earth below, like Cain or Esau, but lift my soul to Her Most Holy Heart to become an heir too by receiving, like Jacob, heavenly blessings." * — come, let your thoughts be on heavenly things now so that you will be able to comprehend what Wisdom is hiding from you; for this you need self-abasement and repentance; the mystery that had been hidden for generations is now being revealed to you; your hope of salvation

All this was like a confession given to us by Jesus so that we say it.

62

is at your hand's reach; have you not noticed how, in these end of times, the Queen of Peace is passing over the earth, escorted by My Angels? have you not noticed how Her Immaculate Heart is proclaiming My Word to you all and preparing My Reign? have you not noticed how your Blessed Mother's Heart is training Her children and forming them Heart to heart so that everyone is ready for My Reign? have you not noticed how, from Her Treasury, She is per-

63

fecting you in Her Heart for Me? I have given the Queen of Heaven and earth all the jewels of Wisdom in Her Heart, and from this treasury She gives abundantly Her graces to take you out of the power of darkness and make you great saints and apostles, and great warriors to join Her in this great battle of your times; with Her Maternal love, the Queen of Heaven seeks all ways to obtain your freedom so that you gain heaven; She instructs you and reminds you that

64

you, too, are Her child, belonging by grace to the imperial household of the Saints in heaven and that She reserved for you, too, a throne among the Saints; — there is nothing I cannot do for the Delight-of-My-Heart*[1] because from the beginning there was nothing in Her that would see things differently from the way My Father, I, and the Holy Spirit would see them; Our*[2] Will was in perfect union with Her will; Her desires were Our desires; for I am

*[1] Mary, Our Blessed Mother
*[2] Holy Trinity

Excerpts from Notebook 84

3 April 96 continued from NB #83, p.64...How could your heart have taken such a deceptive path to abstain from Her intercession?

9 April 96, NB p.4 (Our Blessed Mother speaks): ...The Lord, in His Mercy has given you this Treasure (the Message: 'True Life in God') directly from His Sacred Heart

✠ To this day His glory shines on the lowly, and He will continue to send the rich empty away

✠ Honour your Mother's Heart by refusing evil; do good and entreat your Father in heaven for the gifts of His Spirit

✠ I want you perfect for Immanuel's Heart;...your heart too will become an altar for the Most High

✠ Our Two Hearts pursue the sinners untiringly...but so many...make a mockery of Our Calls

✠ The angels themselves would have liked to be in your place

✠ If rebellion against all the Holy Rules of God has reached its peak...it is because your generation refused to listen to My Words

✠ The Father's Hand will fall on you...and in a tempest of fire He will execute judgment

✠ Very soon now, Our Hearts, which are united into One, will triumph and many things that We foretold will be accomplished...

15 April 96, NB p.17...I will scatter the apostates

✠ The prophets who prophesy falsely...go by unhindered; whereas My Own prophets...are being disabled and persecuted

✠ Many priests equip themselves for war to go against the Vicar of the Church

✠ Satan's hour is here

✠ Soon My Voice will he heard like a clap of thunder...saying "Enough! Enough is enough!"

✠ For those who never feared Me, that Day, they will learn to fear Me

✠ Tell this remnant of Mine that every attempt should be made to lessen My wrath

✠ Fury grips Me when I see the Blessed Sacrament of My Son trampled underfoot

May 96, NB p.35 (Spain)...Do not leave one stone unturned so that the Father and I will not say one day: 'you have not tried your best'

23 May 96, NB p.37 (Alexandria, Egypt)...Realize how happy I am when all of you pray in one voice to Me

✠ Little things please Me and become great in My Eyes

13 June 96, NB p.38...Happy the nations who consecrate themselves to My Sacred Heart

✠ There is only a short time left now and no one can evade My Hour; remember, I am your Shelter

3 July 96, NB p.42...I will draw all of you who want into an intimate union with Me...into a greater interiour life and higher forms of prayer

✠ Many of you have made out of My Kingdom a Kingdom of words alone; I tell you: My Kingdom is Power

4 July 96, NB p.50...A dear brother of Mine disowns Me openly

✠ Raise your eyes to see greater things that are to come

8 July 96, NB p.52...Wisdom will provide you with sound teaching

✠ You shall soon be seeing Me face to face

12 July 96, NB p.55...Anyone who claims to 'inherit' this Message is deluded and deceived by Satan

✠ I have blessed this work which will provide the Church good fruit

13 July 96, NB p.57...You have the Perfect Visitor, standing at your doorstep

✠ Place your head on My Sacred Heart and obtain the delights of My Heart

15 July 96, NB p.60...Let them know that I am <u>their</u> Father and that all of you are the work of My Love

I

the Heart of Her Heart, the Soul of Her Soul, the Spirit of Her Spirit; have you not heard of Our Oneness in Heart, Soul and Spirit? – My state on earth, as God-Man, was divine, yet I was obedient, living under the authority of My Mother and My Adoptive Father; I emptied Myself to assume the condition of a slave by accepting death, and you, generation, have not yet understood that the True Vine cast His roots

2

in the Vineyard*[1] of My Father, and the Spouse of the Holy Spirit, the City of God*[1], the Promised Land, is your Mother too in whom you owe honour; ah, generation, how could your heart have taken such a deceptive path to abstain from Her intercession? have you not read: "the Lord God will give Him the throne of His ancestor David?"*[2] the Queen of heaven and earth is My Throne too; She is the Throne of

*[1] Our Blessed Mother. *[2] Lk 1:32

3

your King, who was made flesh from David's line .... the Lord your God, "would rule over the House of Jacob forever and ever and His Reign will have no end".* the Jacobs of today are Her children, the apostles of the end of times, and the great Saints that through My Mother's Heart are raised and formed, to be one heart with Us forever and ever, for My Reign in their heart will have no end; ♡ be one;

* Lk 1:33

A Ω

4

9. 4. 96

- Our Blessed Mother -

My Vassula, listen to Me very carefully now: the Lord, in His Mercy has given you this Treasure* directly from His Sacred Heart, He has shown the power of His Arm by bringing this good news to the ends of the earth; if all of you only knew what the Lord is offering you in your times! but the Spirit of the Lord will come only to the simple and to the pure of heart and

* The Message: 'True Life in God'

5

fill them with His gifts; to this day His glory shines on the lowly, and He will continue to send the rich empty away.... through this Message He is calling you to a life of Peace; God is calling all of you, for He is Father; He is calling you to amend your lives and live holy; I, your Mother, bless all those who returned to God and I praise Him whose Mercy reaches from age to age, whereas those who continue to rely on _their_ philosophy obstinately, leading an immoral life, pray and fast

6

for them, My Heart, as a Mother is torn by their refusal and by their blindness .... ah!, what pain, what thorns in My Heart, my child! and you, continue to testify in the Name of the Father, My Son, and the Holy Spirit; continue to make Their Name known and go wherever the Father, My Son and the Holy Spirit tell you to go; They will not fail you, so trust in Them; My daughter, I am always where Jesus is; We are with you, so do not fear; Love will conquer in the end ....

7

do not be afraid of the proud of heart for although they boast of their power, they are nothing in the Lord's Eyes; have you not heard: "the Lord of All does not cower before a personage, He does not stand in awe of greatness..."*[1] "ruthless judgement is reserved for the high and mighty; the lowly will be compassionately pardoned,"*[2] and He will continue to rout the proud of heart.... in these days

*[1] Ws 6:7
*[2] Ws 6:6

8

Jesus has revealed to you My Heart; learn, My daughter, that I have inscribed your name in My Heart; I have done the same for all those who love My Son and love Me; honour Me with sacrifices, honour My Heart with the innocence of a child, honour your Mother's Heart by refusing evil; do good and entreat your Father in heaven for the gifts of His Spirit; grow in My Immaculate Heart and I will remedy all the wounds* of your soul, so that you

* this is to be understood as 'sins'.

9

can become the Joy of Jesus, your Saviour, and the twilight of this dark generation; grow in your Mother's Heart, so that your whole being glitters like some precious stones with the Light* I am enveloped with, that hordes of nations will come then to you, attracted by your beauty*2 and when they will ask: "who modelled you to be glittering like a thousand gems?" testify and say: "I was modelled within

*1 Our Lady means, the Holy Spirit.
* In Our Lady's Heart our soul can be embellished but we are without merit.

10

the Purest of Hearts, taking shape in this same Heart our Redeemer blossomed and took flesh and blood, so that I become the child of the Mother of God too; in this way I would be able to express thoughts worthy of the Almighty's gifts;" come, and grow in My Heart and become the heart of My Heart; - draw from My Heart all the Riches I have been given from Wisdom so that you too can learn to love the Father, My Son and the Holy Spirit; in this way you will be the child of

11

the Mother of God; come, come and draw from My Heart the virtues I have been given*, they are for you too, My child, ah, I want you beautiful for My Son, and pleasing to the Father, I want you perfect for Immanuel's Heart; I will pour from My Immaculate Heart into your heart, My child, all My graces so that your heart too will become an altar for the Most High, a censer filled with burning incense, so that you too will walk with

* Created without sin, from the beginning.

12

Grace and Faithfulness; the mystery of God can be revealed only to the pure of heart and if Our Two Hearts pursue the sinners untiringly it is because of the greatness of the love We have for all of you; ah, but so many do not seem to understand or care, and make a mockery of Our Calls; when this time of Mercy will be over, the dead will not come to life*; Our Two Divine Hearts are wounded and are crying out with pain to all of you to amend, to pray, to fast and

* It means, it will be too late to change once this time of Mercy is over.

13

truly to love My Son in the Blessed Sacrament; I invite you to step in My Heart and I will hide you, I will guard you and protect you from all evil surrounding you and from the temptations; I will protect you and lift you, My child, from the tempestuous waters of sin and hide you in My Motherly Heart; My love and My affection for you are so great that the angels themselves would have liked to be in your place; the Sacred Heart of Jesus has no favourites but neither has Mine,

14

God is just and good; today, daughter, and in the following days you will be in the Holy week of Jesus' Passion for the second time*, you realize how Our Two Hearts feel for your division ....
Our injuries to Our Two Hearts are innumerable; if the flock of the Lord is divided and dispersed, and the land reduced into a desert; if rebellion against all the Holy Rules of God has reached its

* The Roman Catholic Easter was from 4-8 April
The Orthodox Easter, from 11-15 April

15

peak, if today Cardinal goes against Cardinal, Bishop against Bishop and priest goes against priest, it is because your generation refused to listen to My Words; I was sent by the Most High to warn you and correct you gently,* but to this day your generation refuses Us a place in its heart and does not take Our Words seriously; upon you, you will draw what you have reaped; My Motherly Heart grieves to tell you this, and My Eyes weep Tears of blood, at the sight I see before Me,

* At Fatima ? Akita ?

16

when the Father's Hand will fall on you with a thundering cry: "enough! enough now!" and in a tempest of fire He will execute judgement .... Our Two Pierced Hearts are still solemnly warning you and We will persist in warning you to change your hearts and turn them towards God; only in God one can live, for He is Your daily bread, your drink and your breath..

let all the inhabitants of Our Two Hearts know that very soon now, Our Hearts, which are united into One,

17

will triumph and many things that We foretold will be accomplished ♡ the Sacred Heart of Jesus and My Immaculate Heart bless all of you; be one; ♡

15.4.96

The fools say in their heart,
'There is no God!'
They are false, corrupt, vile,
there is not one good man left.

God is looking down from heaven
at the sons of men,
to see if a single one is wise,
if a single one is seeking God.
Ps 53:1-2

18

I, Yahweh give you My Peace; I look down from heaven, and I see plundering in My House, but I will scatter the apostates so do not let your courage run low .... never forget who raised you up; it is I who have taken you out of your crib and who, like a tender mother carrying her child to her bosom carried you and nursed you so that your up-bringing would be solely done in My Courts ...! My Will was your daily bread and it is in this same way

19

I shall continue to feed you; you fear without reason, am I to say that you do not trust Me anymore? I allow Me to remind you of your incapacity and your inability to do whatsoever without Me; I admit that, although I am Father to you, I am also your Archer and I have you as one of My favourite targets, just so as to keep your spirit available for Me and well-disposed, devout, I want you; this is why I will continue to aim My arrows at you .... hear Me,

20

although many are fighting against you, do not fear, they will not overcome you, because I am with you; Vassula, although the tempest blown by My Enemy*, full of threats, is blowing on you, do not fear, I am with you; in your days, the prophets who prophesy falsely, trumpeting all sorts of falsehoods, go by unhindered; whereas My Own prophets who come from My Mouth, who openly declare the Truth, My Law and how

* God means Satan

21

your generation apostatized and is well on its way to perdition, unless I hear from them a cry of repentance, they are being disabled and persecuted .... I have kept silent and have shut My Eyes so far, I have drawn back many times My Hand from falling upon you, generation, and so many times I have receded My decisions to redress you by fire; but how could I keep silent at the sight of this Abomination that My prophet Daniel spoke of ? hear Me: in your days, many priests

22

equip themselves for war to go against the Vicar* of the Church; those very ones who teach whatever they please and the world loves it! they are full of compromises to please the world they would sell My Son's Blood! how can I see what I see and remain silent? when they hear My Voice through My prophets, their hands fall limp, and do not take it as an alarm or as a heavenly sign; whereas the priests who are sound and are as Jacob, yielding at

* Pope John Paul II

23

their Mother's authority, I will betroth them for ever to Myself; I will betroth them to Myself and they will be called sons of the Most High; Satan's hour is here; he swore from the day I raised you, daughter, to silence you; he puts all his fury against you, but I tell you, if you remain modest and without ambitions and if you maintain your vow of faithfulness to Me, to My Son, to My Holy Spirit and to your Mother of Perpetual Help, he will shrivel away from you;

24

continue to be all that he is not; My Words in your mouth will continue to be like fire for all those* who, in their apostasy raise My Son's Body and Blood not only without fear, but also without faith they raise him with treachery!

How long until Your Son's return? *[2]

you have no right to ask Me, Vassula, then on the other hand you are still learning and I love you; but there is one thing I am willing to share

*[1] God means the priests *[2] I asked out of desperation, without though

25

with you and I will deprive you not of this knowledge: soon My Voice will be heard like a clap of thunder; I will be heard saying: "enough! enough is enough!" the earth will rent and those who rebelled against Me will see My Hand falling on them; but the vessels of My Son, I will uphold; I will come in a tempest of fire; for some, this will come as a blessing, but for those who never feared Me, that Day, they will learn to fear Me.... to this very day, they have

26

not learnt to venerate My Name and adore Me; they never ask themselves whether they are on the right road, nor do they consult My Spirit for advice, they have become like merchants going into My Sanctuary and out of My Sanctuary, buying and selling in My Son's Name... O evil inclination, earth so defiled! why have you*, who consecrated yourself

* Consecrated souls who apostatized.

27

to My Son's ministry, turned against Him, selling His Body and Blood? return to the service of My Son and I will make you a wonder to the souls, those very souls you drag along with you to perdition; come and repent and I will revive your spirit and brighten your eyes to see the Glory of My Spirit, He who will keep you where you ought to have been from the beginning of your ministry; come, approach Me now so that I breathe in your tent and you will

28

inhale life; My daughter, tell My people, tell this remnant of Mine that every attempt should be made to lessen My wrath; encourage My people, tell them that if they pray with their heart for the conversion of the world, I, Yahweh, their Eternal Father, will reward them for eternity; 'since mercy and wrath alike belong to Me who am mighty to forgive and to pour out wrath, My Mercy is great, but My severity is as great'*;

* Si: 16:11-12

29

I look at the earth today and wish I never did .... My Eyes see what I never wanted to see and My Ears hear what I dreaded to ever hear! My Heart, as a Father sinks with grief; I fashioned man in the likeness of My Image, yet they have degraded themselves and today, so many of them have taken the likeness of the Beast! their heart is so filled with lust, lawlessness, arrogance and perversion! their mouth is accustomed to cry out high and low abusive words; they swear against

30

all heaven to make war against Me and against My Son .... ah.... they do all that My Heart detests; very often My Hand reaches out to My Cup that brims over with My Justice ....!

(Later on)

tell Me, daughter, I call from on high, I do not call to startle you but to advise you; I love you .... write: (continuation of message).

Satan today has stretched his hand all the way to reach the sacerdotal souls,

31

a spirit of lethargy and misconception is looming over those he has touched;* they raise My Son's Body without faith in them, without real praise and all day long they twist My Words and the Tradition of the Church; how can I remain silent when I see how these priests have become Satan's prey? how can I not warn all of you of their movements? are these to go by unpunished for such a crime?

Help us in this hour of crisis ....

* *Tempted*

32

I, for My part, have opened the heavens to help you; I am pouring out My Spirit upon those who invoke My Holy Spirit to come and counsel them, but as I open the doors of heaven and rain down My gifts on humanity and I use the winds as messengers too, the earth rejects My gifts and My messengers, defiling both of them; I display signs and wonders, but the earth again fails to appreciate the fruits of My great Love.... fury grips Me when I see the Blessed Sacrament of My Son trampled underfoot, when I know, that still, to this day, in spite of your wickedness, generation, My Son would lay down His Life, all over again, at once for you, if that were necessary! He* opens His Mouth panting with pain and His Eyes never cease streaming with tears, disappointed with His Own for allowing evil to overpower them; how remote these are from the Truth.... and yet.... in spite of all their iniquity, My Son attends them lovingly, for there is no

* Jesus Christ

34

fathom to His Love; daughter, must I put up with that abomination?* today their bodies are doomed to death, unless I hear a cry of repentance from their heart; come, daughter, persevere in your duty, and do good, and be My Echo; I, Yahweh, bless you;

* Of which the prophet Daniel spoke.

35

Spain - May - 96

My Lord?

I Am; lean on Me, in My Sacred Heart find My Peace which I give to you ♡ remember, I am with you; daughter, do not leave one stone unturned so that the Father and I will not say one day: 'you have not tried your best'; favour above all, all those whose heart is as far from Me as the earth is from the sky; take My mighty Hand and do not fear; all those who want to hear will hear;

36

come; IC -

pray, pray, pray; it is not difficult to pray; Vassula, say: 'Christ is risen!'

I should say it as the custom wants.*[1]

yes! say it now*[2].... and so I have;

delight Me and praise Me! flower, My own daughter of My Church, your Christ is indeed risen; come, I bless you and all those whom I have chosen to

*[1] For 40 days after Easter, the Orthodox has it in their tradition to greet each other with: 'Christ is risen', the response is: 'Truly He has risen.' Jesus wanted me to follow this tradition.

*[2] I said it.

accompany you; they shall have their reward in the end; My Father and I bless those hearts and tell them: spread Our Messages, they save....

Egypt - Alexandria - 23.5.96

My Lord?

I Am; ah! I am well pleased with you for having understood Me; My child, realize how happy I am when all of you pray in one voice to Me, offering Me your time; realize how happy I am when

38

you and I share everything; all I ask is love; dearest souls, keep Me always in your mind and I am glorified in that way; remember, little things please Me and become great in My Eyes; so feel loved by Me; I and you, you and I, united in love; I, Jesus, bless you for the hour of adoration given to Me; have My Peace; ic

13. 6. 96

Happy are those who keep Your ways,
Blessed, whoever listens
to Your Heartbeats,
for they bring Life ...

39

peace be with you, My little one, you are in My Heart, so speak without fear, listen to My Spirit and write:

happy the nations who learn to acclaim My Sacred Heart! they will live in the light of My favour,

happy the nations who consecrate themselves to My Sacred Heart; O what will I then not do for them! I will keep My promise and they will see My Throne one day; I had sworn on My Holiness to keep them secure in My Heart and

40

so I will ... I never fail in My faithfulness and you, be My delight in My assemblies and do not fear; there is only a short time left now and no one can evade My Hour; remember, I am your Shelter; I make your home in My Sacred Heart part never from Me; I love your sighs of thirst for Me, your God; I bless you pray for the unrepentant; I love them too as much as I love you; My love for you is fathomless; remember, I Am is with you and for always;

41

renew yourself in My Spirit, I Am is your Consoler and your Drink; He is your Bread; what gain, is it for anyone to win the whole world and every treasure it contains and forfeit his life? eat Me and come and drink Me, greater treasure I cannot offer you than this; I tell you in all truth: you have no life in you if you do not eat Me and drink Me; I am the Bread of Life; My Spirit is upon you, be blessed in My Holiness ic

42

3. 7. 96

Are You the One who flashes Your Light in our hearts?

I Am;

Are You, Shaddai, whom we considered so far beyond our reach, that now show Yourself to us, You who are clothed in fearful splendour?

behold! I Am;

Theme, and Song of my life, are You really doing something that exceeds our knowledge and understanding?

I Am; I am fulfilling My Promise ♡

Ointment of my eyes, am I seeing right? are You, in Your faithful Love despatching from above Your Holy Spirit

43

I Am, yes! how much more could I have spoken? Vassula, you see? I am coming down to be with you; My beloved ones, the Father said: He will keep neither the records nor take account in His books*, but He will send you an outpour of His Holy Spirit quicker than planned; why, the Evil one is challenging My Power and his threats are pouring down against My Church; so why do I have to delay or keep silent anymore? now, I, Myself, will challenge

* Meaning dates.

him with the Power of My Holy Spirit and draw each one of you into My Sacred Heart; I will draw all of you who want into an intimate union with Me, so that many of you will be favoured with the mystery of your Salvation, which is, My Cross I will enwrap your soul and keep you thus, in perfect union with Me; and by grace I shall draw from you greater sacrifices, greater amendments; I shall draw you into a greater interiour life and higher forms of prayer ... and, just as the Son of Man did not come to be served but to serve, I will teach you too, to do the same and you, little child, bear My Cross of Unity together with Me and allow yourself to be guided by My Spirit, He will be the Sign for you and your guarantee* that you come from Me; My favour rests upon you; — I still have many favours in store for you, generation, favours that will lead you

* I also heard 'guarantor'

46

into sanctity and into My Kingdom; so I tell you, you who would be ready to judge, do not start judging according to appearances, prematurely, let your judgement mature and be according to what is good and right; – today I cry out as I once did in Jerusalem: 'if anyone is thirsty, come! let him come to Me! come and drink, you who believe in Me! for from My Sacred Heart flows fountains of living water! come and refresh yourselves,

47

come and revive! then, the light of your eyes will become the light of My Spirit; - many of you have made out of My Kingdom a Kingdom of words alone; I tell you: My Kingdom is Power;* I will visit anyone who thirsts for Me in one way or another, and with great power I will restore My Kingdom ♡

I thank You that You are pouring out Your Riches, Your Gifts and Your Favours on us, O Lord!

With the Power of Your Spirit,

* allusion to: 1 Co 4:20

48

You will destroy the wisdom of the wise and bring to nothing all the learning of the learned; You will scatter the philosophers and bring them down;

O Holy One, come! demonstrate the Power of Your Power;*[1] demonstrate the Power of Your Holy Spirit, demonstrate the Power of Your Goodness, demonstrate the Power of Your Faithfulness, Your Intimacy, Your Joy, and Your Love;

Leavened we must become;*[2] grant us then this favour, O Lord, grant us this favour to overpower evil, and get rid of all the old yeast of evil and wickedness that still remains

* Meaning: 'demonstrate the Power of Your Kingdom'. *[2] Allusion to Lk 13:20 'Parable of the yeast'.

49

in us, by replacing it by a fresh batch of yeast!

listen: My Spirit will wield His Great Authority over many nations and adjudicate between many people;* this will be done to fulfill the words when I asked you to prophesy;

Goodness is with you! never doubt .... seek Me always, it pleases Me; seek Me always, it pleases Me; let your hand remain in Mine and you shall not wander astray....

* Is 2:4

I bless you;

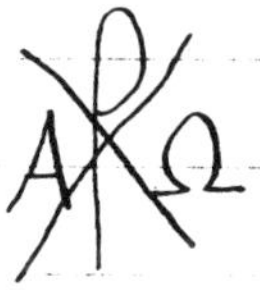

4.7.96

peace be with you; I said: I will come in flaming fire; stand firm and pray with confidence; listen My child: I know you have been deprived from writing but this was done to pay the debt of those who wronged Me; a dear brother of Mine disowns Me openly and so very often ... he grieves My Holy Spirit with his harshness; I set a child by his side;

51

with great confidence I brought My child to him, ah.... how can he fail to see Me in My child whom I raised from the dead? how much longer am I to put up with him? why does he ruin his very self? My garments are spattered with blood, My flesh is ripped from the scourge, and I lie <u>by his side</u> tormented and in agony.... and you, My Vassula, bear this Cross for Me so that you will not lack; better offer you could not have.... My Father will

52

raise your eyes to see greater things that are to come; I Jesus honoured you with My Cross, daughter, have My Peace; I bless you; Wisdom is by your side; I Am;

8. 7. 96

Lord?

I Am; never fall into temptations again ... make My Messages your life's delight; make them known; I am by your side and Wisdom will

53

provide you with sound teaching .... fruit of My Heart, fruit of My Mercy, I, the Lord, will help you; nevertheless, your counsellor ...* never forget that I am in you and you in Me; share your difficulties, your race is not over; I have given you a noble work to both of you; to you, My flower, I have given you this Message, then I have also given you spiritual gifts; I have provided you

* for descretion this was omitted.

54

with graces and favours and as I have done wonders to the first fruits*, and showed My glory in them, so it will be with you too, I will show My glory and the power of My Holy Spirit when you will allow Me to engulf you in Me; and to your counsellor whom I raised for My glory and for My motives, I have given you to him <u>to be counselled</u>; I have given you to him that he may <u>encourage you</u>,

* The Apostles

console you, and look after you with care; you shall soon be seeing Me face to face together with the one I have placed by your side; be concerned now to live for My motives bringing to Me as many souls as possible; repair My broken altars; grace is upon you; come  ΙΧΘΥΣ 

12. 7. 96

(After having heard rumours that some claim that "Jesus" told them that they will be the continuation or 'heirs' of this work: 'True Life in God'.)

56

My Vassula, anyone who claims to 'inherit' this Message is deluded and deceived by Satan; so open your eyes and watch! nobody, after you, will receive a 'continuation' of 'True Life in God' messages; the Messages of this Work will end up with you, when I lift you to Me; anyone, therefore, who claims to be the 'heir' of this work, adding anything to it, know that he does not come from Me. I have blessed this work which will provide the Church good fruit; Jesus Christ is My Name; the Living One who provides Life, is speaking to you now; be blessed;

A Ω

13. 7. 96

Come Lord in the inner place
of Your home;

Come to my table, Lord, so
that You may bless what we will
be sharing, side by side;

Come Lord and fence me in,
behind and in front, in Your Sacred Heart
fence me in;

Let Your Light then cover me,

58

and wrap itself around me, so that there will be never any darkness within me or around me;

Come Faithful Visitor and visit me, now; — see? God will be visiting me now....

I Am is with you; I give you My Peace; your Visitor asks you: do you know of anyone who surpasses My Beauty and My Perfection? no, there is no one .... nor is there anyone who surpasses My Wisdom advice and understanding; you have the Perfect Visitor, standing at your doorstep; you have, indeed, invited at your table now the Alpha and the Omega, the Upright One, who will, not only come in the inner place of your home to share a meal at your side, but will also light your lamp; now, come, lean on Me and satisfy My thirst for souls; contrary to what you may think, your pleas are not in vain; ah.... My Vassula, I am also your Shepherd, so place your head on My Sacred Heart and obtain the delights of My Heart so that you will be more willing

60

than ever before to expiate for your brothers and sisters .... fear not, child of My Father, I will direct you as I always have; come, we, us? I, Jesus Christ, Son of God and Saviour, will sanctify My remnant with My Holy Spirit;

15. 7. 96

My God, grant me to speak as Wisdom wishes us to speak;

Grant me, my Father, the guidance of Wisdom, so that I graciously pass on the riches of Your Kingdom without reserve, to my brothers

61

and to my sisters;

* My daughter, it is your Father speaking; Yahweh is My Name; — since your heart yearns to speak words of Wisdom and understanding, to reveal My Holiness and the riches of My Kingdom, I will grant you this favour so that hordes of nations may listen to My Voice and get to know Me and understand that I am Father; yes, let them know that I am <u>their</u> Father and that all of you are

* The Father speaks

62

the work of My Love;

My Yahweh is great and supremely to be praised, yes! let my lips have wisdom to utter words only for *His* Glory, let my heart seek only sound sense and my mind absorb His sweet conversation so that Your Love, Father, which is as high as heaven, be known to the unknown, so that they too will rejoice and walk in Your Presence for ever and ever!

learn that anyone of you who turns to Me with the sole desire to please Me, with all My Heart, yes, with all My Heart, I will grant him My favours.... I will reveal to them My Image of

Excerpts from Notebook 85

15 July 96, continued from NB #84 p.62...I will breathe out a scent like incense upon My creation...as never before in history

✠ I want to heal your apostasy and give you all a pure heart so that you need not avoid Me in shame

17 July 96, NB p.9...Like a clap of thunder, I shall descend upon you to give you freedom and bring you in union with Our Oneness

✠ I will come upon those who never sought Me yet their hearts remained as those of children

✠ Come to Me in fear and trembling and I will make you a fearless warrior of your times

✠ So will I pour out My Presence on all mankind

2 August 96, NB p.20...I have created man to utter words of wisdom and knowledge

4 August 96, NB p.23...Why do you keep yourselves bound on these disordered worldly inclinations that attack your soul?

12 August 96, NB p.27..."May Yahweh show His Face and bring you peace;" this is how they must call down My Name

19 August 96, NB p.29 (from St. Michael)..."Fear of the Lord"...means hatred of all that is evil and opposite to God

✠ So unless you change your hearts and become free of malice you will never enter into God's kingdom

✠ How can anyone believe that they will escape God's Justice?

✠ Once the Holy One has spoken, His Word will be accomplished and Justice will be done by fire

✠ Ask yourselves: "what will the Day of the Lord mean for me?"

2 September 96, NB p.36...come and pray: "...I will proclaim Your Saving Justice till the end

4 September 96 (St. Paul), NB p.39...like crafty masons build a house, these enemies of the Church too are crafty and cunning in their work of destruction

✠ Let your sole concern be: His Church; I, St. Paul, apostle of our Lord Jesus Christ tell you:...stand firm, remain in the grace of God

20 September 96, NB p.44...Revive My Sanctuary; and comfort those who mourn...tell them that Tender Mercy is visiting you all now, to give you strength in the times of ordeal that are to come

- ✠ The hour of rebellion has come…he and his like wish to abolish My Perpetual Sacrifice…many will acknowledge him and his doctrine
- ✠ My Mother and I are raising disciples who become personal friends to Us and intimate, so that they will stand up like lights on a lamp-stand and shine in those days of ordeal; they will be the sturdy pillars of My church…upheld by My Holy Spirit

23 September 96, NB p.53 ...I will continue to pour My graces on you, to disconcert the wise and the learned of your times

- ✠ My Spirit works in different manners, always for a good purpose
- ✠ Let your spirit be invaded by My Spirit; for this, you have to die to yourself; the humbler you get to be, the easier My Spirit will find its way in you

27 September 96, NB p.56...Do all you can and I will do the rest

- ✠ It pleases Me when your persecutors impose on you impressive wounds…let some of your friends even feel ashamed of your presence…this unfairness pleases Me, for it sanctifies your soul…suffering in My way means bringing you closer to Me, closer to My traits
- ✠ I will send you all over the world to spread my Messages …speak and be My Echo…let us continue having a heart to heart conversation; love Me

Goodness, so that they end their journey with Me; have you not noticed how I despatch My Holy Spirit, carrier of Wisdom, from the holy heavens? what seemed to be for all of you inaccessible and unattainable* will be prompted to descend on you, by My good Will; "deliver us!" some of you plead, "come and fortify us, Father!" I hear as an outcry from My creation; "send us promptly Your Holy Spirit

* God speaks of the Holy Spirit.

2

from above!" others call in their thirst or, "get up! save us!" at these cries I said: "I will breathe out a scent*[1] like incense upon My creation; I will spread My perfume as never before in history; have you not read*[2]: "I, like a conduit from a river, like a watercourse running into a garden, I am going to water My orchard, I intend to irrigate My flower beds; and see,

*[1] God is talking about His Holy Spirit.
*[2] Ecc: B. Sirach: 24:30-33

My conduit has grown into a river, and My river has grown into a sea; now I shall make discipline shine out, and I shall send its light far and wide; I shall pour out teaching like prophecy, as a legacy to all future generations;" and My people will say: "look! look how our Father is advancing like the clouds! look how He is pouring out His Holy Spirit with a Blessing*;" I want to heal your

*Read Nb 6:22-27.
Also receiving special graces & mystical favours while resting in His Spirit.

4

disloyalty, I want to heal your apostasy and give you all a pure heart so that you need not avoid Me with shame;

many of you will stand aghast, perplexed and stupefied, others will harbour doubts in their heart, others will set their faces harder than rock at the powerful Presence of My Spirit; yet, I am only accomplishing My Son's Promise and when people will ask you: "who are these flying like a cloud, like doves to their cote?*" answer and say:

* Is 60:8

5

"these are the sons and daughters who found their freedom in the Spirit, they are those who called out to their Father: 'my Father,' and who are to adorn His Sanctuary once again; they will feed now on the wealth of His Holy Spirit; they are the people whom the Father has blessed; yes! the Holy Spirit, the Giver of Life, will be their splendour, and they will continue to be suckled on the riches of His Holy Spirit...." this is what you

6

will tell My people .... come;

17. 7. 96

(A prayer to the Holy Spirit.)

O Light! O Inaccessible Light,
thrice Holy,

Come! descend now and come not
only on those who invoke You
because they have heard of You,
but come also on those who
have never known You!

Come! O Lamp of our body!
Come and correct all those who
have never understood You;

Come to all those who fear You,
Come and unveil Your hidden treasures,
these treasures kept for our times,

Come! come and reveal the Father
and the Son's Holy Countenances,
Come and reveal Yourself, Holy Spirit!
Come my Friend,
for You are the dazzling Light
of our heart,
Come from on high and clothe us
with Your power and splendour;

Come and lodge inside us and
make out of Your Dwelling,
a place of prayer, for
You are the Constant Prayer;

See how naked we are now without
You?
Come and shine Your Light in this
darkness;
You are The Promise,

8

You are our Love,
You are our Light,
Yes! You <u>are</u> <u>The Promise</u>!

You are the One of whom Scriptures say:
"It will never be night again and they will not need lamplight or sunlight, because the Lord God will be shining on them." (Ap. 22:5)

You are our Pledge of our inheritance,
Holy be Your Name and Blessed;
You are the priceless and inestimable pearl;
You are the radiance of our soul,
You are The Banquet and our festivity,
You are the Irresistible Companion of our life,
You are the Throne of the poor in spirit,
You are the Kingdom of Kingdoms,
the Empire of the empires,

9

O Visitor of our soul,
Come and free us!
Amen

My child*, prayer is your weapon, and I, I can take you out of the power of darkness to place you into what you once thought of Me: the Inaccessible Light and the Unattainable Treasure; in My Glorious Power, My child, you can obtain your strength, your gentleness and your patience; you can obtain perseverance and in Me and through

* The Holy Spirit speaks.

10

Me, you can call out: "Amen!" and I, The Amen, the Faithful One, the True Witness, the Ultimate Source of God's creation, will hear you! like a clap of thunder, I shall descend upon you to give you freedom and bring you in union with Our Oneness, filling you with the absolute fullness of Our Trinitarian Holiness ♡

a baptism of Fire is coming upon you, creation! a baptism so longed for, to make all things new again

11

daughter, proclaim the Kingdom of God and let no one hinder you*[1] .... ask for the Fountain of Living Water, to come upon you like a Spring to refresh you!

Hope of hopes, can I really ask You to unchain those that are still chained?

<u>ask</u>! have you not heard that freedom is to be found in Me*[2]? I tell you, I will come upon those who never sought

*[1] I think this was said like: "No one will be able to stop the Kingdom being proclaimed.

*[2] The Holy Spirit.

12

Me, yet their hearts remained as those of children; I will reveal My glorious power to those who never even consulted Me, I will go where I am not banned; - the time of sorting out has come; the time to reveal the glorious riches of the Kingdom has come; the time of grace is upon you; this is why I tell you again: you, who make part of Christ's Body, come, and <u>aspire</u> for My gifts so that you may <u>fully</u> penetrate into the Mystery of Christ; and do not be

13

like the apostates who stopped looking for what is right; — and you who say to the ones who invoke Me:* 'this prayer is not in my domain', I ask you: 'is it possible that you did not hear Me? could it be that you did not see Me? is it possible that you did not understand Me? am I now to say that you are resisting Me? you claim to have knowledge of Me but the things

* Invoking the Holy Spirit while laying hands on people.

14

you say and do are nothing but a denial of My graces; —* peace be with you; survivor of this great Apostasy, glorify Our Name thrice Holy and intimately give Us praise;

(The Holy Spirit then opened my mouth and filled it with praises for God.)

I give thanks and praise
to the awe-inspiring Lord,
so stupendously great;

Look! the One who flashes His Rays
dazzling my eyes, is none other but
my Father!

* The Holy Spirit of God then addressed me once more.

15

O Brilliant Adornment
of the Heavens!
The greatness of Your Name
liberated me,
and by raising my ear just a little,
I received Your Word
from Your Mouth;

and now:
I sing for joy to God,
my Father!

I shout in triumph to the Anointed One,
Jesus Christ, my Saviour!

My Promised One,*
O Delight of the delights! I love You
for making me Your friend;

and now, I call out with all my heart:

* Allusion to Eph. 1:13

16

"Amen! my zeal is burning me up
to announce and proclaim
Your Faithful Love!

I shall do Your Will and I shall
bring as many as possible
in union with Your Oneness,
so that they too will be filled
with the absolute fulness of
Your Trinitarian Holiness."

Amen.

may your ways remain steady in doing
Our Will; in your days, I am
the stone which the builders reject, yet,
I am the cornerstone of the Church;
liberty and love is to be found in Me
and yet, I am rejected by your generation

for they have not understood Me .... they hardly consult Me .... look, I am like a rich soil; if you sow your seeds in Me, your harvest will be: Eternal Life  and Paradise will be your home; come to Me without delay and I will make you rich, through your poverty; strong, through your weakness; zealous and faithful, through your wretchedness; a living Altar for Our Trinitarian Holiness, through your nothingness; come to Me in fear and trembling and I will

18

make you a fearless warrior of your times to join Saint Michael and his army*[1] and fight in the great battle of your times; — I am an unceasing prayer in you and where you lack, I fill, always accessible to the poor and the simple; come and seize Me.... come and possess Me and I will mould you into My Holiness*[2] offering you My Inestimable gifts, making you part of Us*[3] and one in Us to go and rebuild

*[1] I heard at the same time: 'angels.'
*[2] I heard also at the same time: 'Deity.'
*[3] Holy Trinity

the ruins of Our Sanctuary; — you who have come from the desert, come and step into My deep waters and My waves will wash over you and refresh you; do not fear Me, have you not heard, My friend, that I will change the dry land into a sea? for from the heavens I will pour out on you My gifts and My favours; just like the heavens pelt down rain at the Presence of Our Trinitarian Holiness, so will I pour out My Presence on all mankind; — meditate upon

20

this; we, us? ____________

Yes, forever.

2. 8. 96

I love You, Lord;
I will thank Your Name once again,
since You are my God,
my Friend and my All;
I thank You for all Your mysteries,
I thank You for the wonder of
Your Works,
I thank You for Your Salvation Plan;

Let us all celebrate our
King's actions!

come, My Vassula, I give you My Peace....
yes, for I have called you to a life of

21

peace; I have created man to reflect My Glory since I have made him in My likeness; I have created man to utter words of wisdom and knowledge; I have created him to obtain the gifts of My Holy Spirit; have you not read: "every gift is for your benefit, so that as grace spreads, so, to My glory, thanksgiving may also overflow among more and more people;" (2 Co 4:15) O creation whom I love to folly! although you are near to death, I am here, to renew you day by day! so then, be

22

rooted in Me now, and overflow with thanksgiving; aspire for the things that are from heaven, where I am and where you belong; let your foundations be rooted in love, faith and hope; keep My Law and the sound teachings I have been givin you; you are living among wolves, My lambs, but My Holy Spirit is with you, to look after you; do not be afraid, I am with you too; stand firm, and do not be afraid; the Father's Eyes are upon you... and We, in

23

Our Trinitarian Holiness will shepherd you till the end .... be one! ΙΧΘΥΣ

4. 8. 96

*Come, let us open a way for
the Rider of the Clouds,
let our prayers be His staircase;*

*Descend now, my Lord and be
with us. Maranatha!*

I give you My Peace; hear Me: My Holy Spirit, thrice Holy, Giver of Life and Throne to the poor in spirit, cries out today: "come! come all you who desire Me and are thirsty for righteousness!

24

you cannot be My child unless you are suckled on My riches! ah! so many of you are bound by the chains of lust and of darkness! yet, My Holy Spirit can fill you where you lack, so that My Word, in all its glory and sovereignty can abide in you.... anyone who has done wrong, come! come and humble yourself and repent, so that My Eyes may delight in you; anyone who is not living holy, come! come to Me and repent! I will give you a new heart;

25

anyone who still is attached to the world cry out to Me and ask Me to unbind your chains! why do you keep yourselves bound on these disordered worldly inclinations that attack your soul? your adornment should be an interiour purity, your adornment should be truthfulness, so that My Holy Spirit will not shy away from you!... woe to you who have lost the strength to endure; (Si 2:14) have you not heard: "those who fear the Lord do their best to please Him;"* (Si 2:16)

26

if you did not know this, come, humble yourself and follow Me and let your love grow in Me so that your heart may never turn away again ♡

ah .... Vassula, My child, say to Me:

'Jesus Christ You are my Life,
You are my Rock,
You are my Salvation,
You are my Archer,'

and I will reply to you:

My child, you are Mine,
you are My seed,

you are My joy,
you are My target, on
which I am thrusting blessing
upon blessing for the sole
purpose: to save you....
come, remember, I am **always** with you!
I, Jesus Christ, bless you all!

ΙΧΘΥΣ 

12. 8. 96

Why does it appear incredible to some who see the Power of Your Holy Spirit, manifesting Himself, even when they rest in the Spirit? I am saying nothing more than words of welcome, entreating and

28

pleading for healing, and for receiving Your gifts.

(I then opened the Bible and read: Nb 6: 22-27

"Yahweh spoke to Moses and said; speak to Aaron and his sons and say: this is how you must bless the Israelites. You will say:

"may Yahweh bless you and keep you,
may Yahweh let His Face
shine on you and
be gracious to you,
may Yahweh show His Face and
bring you peace;"

this is how they must call down My

Name on the Israelites and then I shall bless them;"* — I will blow My blessing on anyone who calls Me, and I will shine on them bringing them peace and I will be gracious to them; so will it be.... let anyone who wishes to drink, let him come to Me and I will bless him!

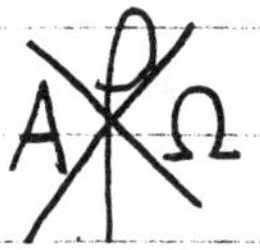

19.8.96

(Saint Michael, the Archangel)

child of the Father and of the Most High,

* God wanted me to write this down in that manner.

30

spouse of the Spouse, garden of the Holy Spirit, fruit of the Most Holy Trinity, do you know what, "fear of the Lord", means? it means hatred of all that is evil and opposite to God; God is good, meek, gentle, merciful, love and the Truth; let your soul then be fearing God and allow God to perfect you; the fear of the Lord is the beginning of Wisdom and Wisdom is given to mere children for it is to such as these that the kingdom of

31

heaven belongs, so unless you change your hearts* and become free of malice you will <u>never</u> enter into God's kingdom; ah.... have you not heard, how Our Creator, thrice Holy, triumphant over all, had wept with tears of joy while He was creating you? yes, it is this same God, who is the Most High, the great and living God, to whom you owe your life, who created you, that the world today has turned

* St Michael speaks now to everyone.

32

against Him; how can anyone believe that they will escape God's Justice? all is for ever under the Eye of God, and what He sees as crimes and offenses on His Holiness outweigh the sands of the seas..... for how long will He see His Image profaned? can man support himself on nothing, and for how long? refusing Faithful Love is to refuse Life; yet the God they have forgotten has never forgotten them; I can now plead for mercy for all of you, especially for those amongst you whose hearts are the hardest; the weak and the needy have to be rescued and saved from the clutches of the evil one, who plots the fall of God's people; so come! revive your prayers to Me and I shall intercede; come! with a single mind to save God's children, come and pray! while I am giving you this warning, there are those who would not listen; - ask for My intercession and I will protect you and defend you from

34

evil and his dominion; – as heaven praises God's wonders, praise, you too, the Most High, your Creator, without ceasing, for who in the skies can compare with the Almighty One? who among the sons of God can rival Him? His Throne like the sun before me cries out: 'Justice!' once the Holy One has spoken, His Word will be accomplished, and Justice will be done by fire!; but for those whose heart was pleasing to God who cried out to Him: "You are my Father, my God the Rock of my salvation!" so will they be made God's first-born, and will not fear in the Day He will come by fire; soon, Yahweh means to pass through among you; let me hear your fervent prayers, then ask yourselves: "what will the Day of the Lord mean for me?" and anyone who conspires evil, will be working for his own ruin; this is why I tell you:

36

come and sow seeds of peace and reconciliation, so that your fruit will be agreable to the Almighty and heaven will be your compensation ♡
Saint Michael, God's Archangel;

2. 9. 96

daughter, I Am is with you, come and pray, say:

ah, my Lord, how awesome You are
You disperse Your enemies like smoke,
Holy be Your Name thrice Holy;

Your uprightness glorifies You
in our wickedness,
Your faithfulness glorifies You
in our unfaithfulness;
let all hearts seek You my Lord,
and call on Your Name;
let the one who never sought You
find You,
so that he too, in Your Presence,
will say:
'in God alone are saving
justice and strength,'

38

in God alone is my life,
my joy and my peace,
with whom can you compare Him?
with whom can you
equate Him?
I have blossomed in His Salvation
and rejoice now in His Great Love,
Glory be to the Highest,
Glory be to my God thrice Holy;"
Lord, there is no
other but You, and I will
proclaim Your Saving Justice

till the end;

Amen;

come, Your Creator, tells you: I am with you; be blessed;

A ☧ Ω

4. 9. 96

I was inspired to pray to St. Paul, because for days he was stuck on my mind, drawing my attention to focus on him. It was like he was pursuing me. I felt him so near me, as when I am about to receive from our Lord His words. Then when I prayed to him, I received St. Paul's words of council:

peace, my sister in the Lord; watch over your group* and never fail to

* prayer group of Rhodos, Greece.

40

encourage them ... let your hearts be holy, let your hearts proclaim a resurrected Christ have Christ as your Theme always; God has called all of you to share His Glory; He favours the humble and the innocent; above all be pure to be able to face the Lord in good conscience; the Spirit of Grace is upon you, and each one of you has received a special grace; these special graces were given to you for the benefit of the Church to proclaim a Resurrected Christ, something in your days considered

41

as untrue; you are to break this barrier of falsehood that is being built; like crafty masons* build a house, these enemies of the Church too are crafty and cunning in their work of destruction; today God is putting the weak and the wretched to combat what is spectacular and great in the eyes of this pining world of Apostasy! the Presence of His Holy Spirit will lift*[2] so many corpses; immorality in your days is the crown of this wicked

* double meaning. *[2] raise, convert.

42

world; but you my friends, who received the Revelation in a brilliant light, persevere to proclaim God's Glory, proclaim a Living Christ and do not fear persecutions, on the contrary, rejoice! what greater favour could the Lord offer you? do not bout when the spear comes; have you not realized its value? enjoy God's Presence instead, enjoy the Presence of His Spirit and be eager to praise Him, since it is in Him that you all live, it is in Him that you move,

43

breathe, it is in Him that you rest* and will Rest eternally one day .... and you, my sister in the Lord, spend more of your time with the Lord, let your sole concern be: His Church; — I, Saint Paul, apostle of our Lord Jesus Christ, tell you: courage and stand firm, remain in the grace of God and enjoy His Presence; I bless you, in the Name of the Father and of the Son and of the Holy Spirit;

be one ....

* Allusion to: Heb 3:7-19

44

20. 9. 96

Eli, I love You.
Judge of the living and the dead,
I give You my heart.
Eternal Father and Prince-of-Peace*
govern me.

Branch-of-The Vine, peace be with you; I will not deprive you of My Voice, I never deprive children of anything they ask of Me no matter how reckless they might be they can always be disciplined and I can always bring them back to reason yes, wretched they may be, but their Faithful King will keep on shining on

* Is 9 : 5

45

them, giving them peace to attain perfection; soul of My Heart*, begotten for this mission, open your heart now and listen to what I have to say: I called you, to work for Me and at the same time bring you joy in your heart; your race is not yet over .... while you race, I am racing too; by your side I am; will you, for My sake endure for just a while longer?

Lord, I have gripped the hem of Your clothes and I will not let go!

* This should be taken just as an expression of intimacy

46

adorn My Sanctuary;* devastation and ruin have penetrated into My Sanctuary; revive My Sanctuary; and comfort those who mourn, they are My people; tell them that in due time I shall act with speed, for My Spirit will be poured out even to the least and the smallest of you will become mighty; you must encourage and strengthen your brothers and sisters; tell them that Tender Mercy

* This command sounded like a clap of thunder. The Lord had changed the tone of His Voice.

47

is visiting you all now, to give you strength in the times of ordeal that are to come, I will attend tenderly to your needs; multiply your prayers, since in these days, rebellion is growing; rebellion comes from Satan who was the first Rebel; blessed is he who believes that the Promise made by Me would be fulfilled! I tell you most solemnly, the hour of rebellion has come, the hour of this one who claims to be so much greater than all that men call 'god', is here,

48

and he is among you, his desire is to enthrone himself in My Sanctuary to kiss in his doctrine ... profaning My Institution of the Eucharist; he and his like wish to abolish My Perpetual Sacrifice, he wishes to break My Covenant and My Law then once this is done, he will flatter many by conferring great honours on them; this is why many will acknowledge him and his doctrine; but My Own, My Jacobs, who know Me, they will stand firm by My side and will oppose him; even today he puts others to take furious action against My holy ones* because he has set his heart to destroy anyone who is holy; now he is hidden, but will stand up at the appointed time to do his evil.... Satan has bound him for many years now.... and you, you must not lose hope; this is why I said: 'blessed is he who believes that the Promise made by Me would be fulfilled....' My Mother and I are raising disciples

* So as to remain hidden

50

who become personal friends to Us and intimate, so that they will <u>stand up</u> like lights on a lamp-stand and shine in those days of ordeal; they will be the sturdy pillars of My Church because they will be upheld by My Holy Spirit who will be their interior power; ah... generation, your apostasies have been many through the years, but greater apostasy than this one, My Church never encountered before .... tell My people not to be afraid, but to place their hope

51

in Me, for the Father and I know their needs; tell those who have not set their heart for Me to set it now on My Kingdom; do not say: 'our Master is taking His time coming'.... I am at your doors!.... but are you ready to receive Me?

Vassula, there is a lot of work to be done, but remember, you will do this work with Me and you will receive My Strength .... so go out and address My people, be My echo resounding ....

I, Jesus Christ, bless you; we, us?

Yes Lord, but one small question, Lord, - 'will You dethrone the Rebel?

yes! I will dethrone the Rebel; this victory will come with fire and how I wish it were blazing already! but My Church must still receive a baptism and how great is My distress till it is over!* this baptism will come from heaven, the clouds will rain it down; have you not read, pupil of Mine, "let the earth open for salvation

*Allusion to Jesus' Passion. Lk 12:49-50

to spring up; let deliverance, too, bud forth which, I, Yahweh, shall create" ....* I did not create chaos and chaos has now set its roots firmly in this world of Apostasy .... come, I am with you;

23. 9. 96

Lord, I thank You for showing me, who is so unworthy, Your Glory.

You spoke, Lord, but the world is not listening;

* Is. 45 : 8

although You are displaying
Your Glory every-where,
the world refuses to see and believe.

How much longer are we to strife?
Deprived of Your Signs we are not,
but, the world, is determined to
destroy its soul.

I have indeed opened My Mouth and spoken, see for yourselves .... but today the world has no thought for its Maker, no heart for its Creator .... but the world's lack of fidelity will not cancel My Fidelity; through the Power of My Spirit, I will reform the unformed; why, everything done in My Spirit, thrice Holy, will be done so as to glorify Us; I will continue to pour My graces on you, to disconcert the wise and the learned of your times; no man was able to value and understand fully My Holy Spirit; My Spirit works in different manners, always for a good purpose; so be eager to bless in the Name of My Holy Spirit; let your conscience be grasped in full union with My Holy Spirit so that what you do be expressed by My Holy Spirit; let your spirit be invaded by My Spirit, for this, you have to die to yourself; the humbler you get to be, the easier My Spirit will find its way in you; we, us? ic

27. 9. 96

I would not have invoked Your Name,
or roused myself to catch hold of You
so as to possess You, my God,
if it was not for Your very Presence,
that saved me.

Yes, who was there to pity my deplorable state if it was not You Yourself?

King, and Sentinel of my soul,
Seal of my heart,
Flame of Salvation,
Mainstay of our soul,
Rabbuni* thrice Holy,

I entreat You and I pray that
You may continue to shine on me,
so that I learn from Your Mouth
and pass on Your Word
without reserve and self-interest

I will grant you to speak in My Name; you will speak as I would wish you to speak .... do all you can and I will do the rest; by offering

* Meaning 'Master' in Hebrew. Jn 20:16

58

Me your time, I, in My turn, will be offering you My jewels, those of your Salvation; I will be offering you, My Cross, My Nails and My Thorned Crown; I hope to see you cheerful.... so that My Power lasts on you, remain weak and powerless; it pleases Me when your persecutors impose on you impressive wounds by their persecutions and insults; let some of your friends even feel ashamed of your presence while with you, because of the notification,

59

while they would call this 'cautiousness'... this unfairness pleases Me, for it sanctifies your soul; come! I am your Friend! your jealous Friend...! so for My sake, accept the hardships,

accept the scourge too; remain weak so that I, I use My Power on you and through you .... <u>never</u> lift your head and act brazen, remain with your head low so that the world continues to see My Head; I, for My part, will polish your soul arduously so that you will

60

witness in My Name with zeal, and will proclaim Me as the Risen Christ; I was not wrong, lowering you, for in having done so, I lifted you to Me; there is no need to be surprised by My Compassion, My infinite Compassion; I am your Saviour, who died out of love for you; this is why I am continuously looking for any opportunity to have your society ridicule you.... but just look, look at all those indignities, all those wounds that

61

have been done on you and on My Heart; My Heart opened even more now for you so that you crawl in Its depths.... Suffering in My way means bringing you closer to Me, closer to My traits, closer to My interests; sufferings that delight Me, bring you zeal, fidelity and ardour to work for Me; I am, as you said, your Rabbuni, thrice Holy and you, you who are My pupil, I tell you: try to discover what I want out of you; I am the Living God

62

and I forgave you, and I became your intimate Friend; I led you into My Kingdom so that you stop worshipping false gods; I have entrusted you with a work beyond your means, so that through the Power of My Holy Spirit, you would be raised; and you grew in My Spirit; you were formed in Him so that you move in Him and grow strong; see what favours I have given you? if you are bold in your speeches, this boldness comes

63

from My Spirit; in return, Vassiliki, to all those favours I have given you, I want a renewed submission to My Will; you will only gain freedom....

I renew my vows to You my Lord and I submit to Your Holy Will my God.

"Alleluia!

Let heaven praise Yahweh:
praise Him, heavenly heights,
praise Him, all His angels,
praise Him, all His armies!

Praise Him, sun and moon,
praise Him, shining stars,
praise Him, highest heavens!

64

Let them all praise the
Name of Yahweh,
at whose command they were created;

Let earth praise Yahweh,
all kings on earth and nations,
princes, all rulers in the world,
young men and girls, " *
everyone, come and praise
our Lord and do
His Holy Will.

by submitting to My Will, I will send you all over the world to spread My Messages .... speak and be My Echo and say nothing more than what you have learnt; I and you, us, let us continue having a heart to heart conversation; love Me ♡ ic

* Taken from Ps 148

Excerpts from Notebook 86

22 October 96, NB p.1...If you remain obedient to My Church, you will not fail Me

- ✠ Today…a huge population from every country is being drawn to worship the Beast…they have accepted his kingdoms and their luxury…deceived by Satan, they promote error, …liberalism and the like, defying the Truth and the Tradition of My Church
- ✠ This deadly poison is affecting My consecrated souls; this is the smoke that penetrated into My Sanctuary
- ✠ My Messages regarding the Beast of John's Revelation are aimed at them
- ✠ Do not be surprised when these powers of hell join forces together to try and prevent you from exercising your prophetic ministry
- ✠ The power of My Holy Spirit who lives in you terrifies them, because My Holy Spirit gives the world the utter conviction that you come from Me
- ✠ I, the Christ, will walk before you so that with My Sceptre I may point out to you the traitors of My Church who need your prayers
- ✠ The day the Rebel will appear,…I will unmask to the nations your entire plan of destruction
- ✠ If they will repent…and swear loyalty in front of My Throne, I will remember the oath that they made with Me when they were ordained

1 November 96, NB p.24...My Lips will keep feeding you and My Heart will keep loving you and consoling you

- ✠ "Will you delight Me, your God, and be like a lily?"

8 November 96 (New York), NB p.31...The Father and I rejoice in them every time they invoke Our Name with love

9 November 96 (Tampa), NB p.32...You are My first-fruits and I want you holy...I bless each one of you; be one!

10 November 96 (Charleston, S.C.), NB p.34...I will reveal the Treasures of My Heart to them...Love is with you

17 November 96 (St Louis), NB p.36...Enjoy these Inexhaustible riches [Treasures]...reserved for your times now and show them to the world...that has grown cold

27 November 96, NB p.38...My aim is to resurrect the dead...to renew My Church

- ✠ My Heart grieves continuously to watch those in My House who...do not work in My Spirit for unification of the dates of Easter
- ✠ Again I am asking you to unite the Easter dates so that My Spirit shines on you with grace and brings My House into one
- ✠ House of the East...you are not allowing My Holy Spirit to nurture you enough
- ✠ I implore you, House of the West...unmask the Evil one by unifying the dates of Easter as in the primitive Church

27 November 96 (Eve of the 11th anniversary of "True Life In God"), NB p.51... Display the riches of My Sacred Heart to every nation

- ✠ Although they are starving for lack of My Word, they believe they are feasting...tell them...the Lord has prepared for them a banquet

28 November 96, NB p.57...I want to draw them into <u>this</u> Heart...that delights to be with the sons and daughters of men

- ✠ Turn your eyes on My Sacred Heart and Its brightness will fill your dark night into the fullness of day
- ✠ The fire from My Heart is the power to give you light in your soul
- ✠ I said: "I shall come to them with My Heart in My Hand and open My Heart like a reservoir and immerse them with My divine Treasures

I

22.10.96

My Lord, Watchman of my soul
Guardian of my heart,
Salvation of my spirit,
Come and burn to the root
in me all that is not You;
Pass through me to revive
what is dead;

Ruler of Kindness, Justice and Integrity,
speak to me, Your daughter!

daughter of My Church, if you remain obedient to My Church, you will not fail Me .... confess your sins often, admitting you are a sinner, so that the Viper, the father of lies, will be unable to deceive you .... in your repentance you will

2

always produce the appropriate fruit: the fruit of love, so come and grow in My love.... come now and write My Message: I tell you solemnly, the man who will thrust himself voluntarily at the Beast's feet, worshipping him and accepting his kingdoms of the world, will be cast into the fires of hell; I want you to pray for these souls, daughter, for they are as precious as you are to Me; see, daughter, although they are your enemies, you must pray for

3

them to be delivered; they do not realize that making the world their friend is making Me, their God their enemy, this is why My Law, My precepts and My Tradition do not appeal to them ....

when I was led by the Spirit out in the wilderness to be tempted by the devil, and the devil showed Me from a very high mountain all the kingdoms of the world, offering them all to Me if I worshipped him, I replied: "be gone Satan! for Scriptures say: 'you must worship

4

the Lord your God and serve Him alone";
today, to My great sorrow, a huge population from every country is being drawn to worship the Beast and he has become for them their ruler and their god, for they have accepted his kingdoms and their luxury; they have become the traders of the earth; yes! they have set their hearts on the fruits of the world; deceived by Satan, they promote error, obsessed with their sins, they promote liberalism and the like, defying the Truth

5

and the Tradition of My Church; the Lie is defying the Truth! ... so I want you to pray for them, daughter, for I love them too; pray, for they are under the influence of evil forces; these dark powers of the underworld are deluding them and interferring in their priestly ministry ... these evil powers of hell are after My consecrated souls to draw them to believe what is untrue; you are well aware of the depths of My Wounds and I have let you know how

6

much I suffer by trickling from your eyes tears of blood*; how could I not suffer when I see My very Own, whom I love dearly, be so utterly deceived and accepting this deadly poison .... this is why I am telling you with insistence: pray for them, and regard them as brothers to you who need correction; today this deadly poison is affecting My consecrated souls; <u>this</u> is the smoke that pene-

* Manifestation that only a few saw on me while I was praying in the Dublin Conference of 19.10.9

7

trated into My Sanctuary; they are breaking the Law of My Church* and their sin will condemn them unless they repent; now they are the gangrene of My Body who listen to My Word but do not obey it; nobody can imagine them irreligious when you see them, but you will always know them by their fruit which is: disobedience; disobedience to this* Law of My Church, disobedience to the Vicar of My Church, disobedience to the Tradition of My Church,

* AAS, 73 / 1981 pp. 240-241

8

- disobedience to My entire Law; frantic persecutors of My messengers who reveal them and their plans to the entire world, promoters of liberalism; persecutors of My Abels*[1] who oppose them and who instruct My lambs in virtue, defending My Law; these*[2] are of whom Scriptures say: "these are the ones who have kept their virginity*[3] and not been defiled with women; they follow the Lamb wherever

[1]* Consecrated souls who please our Lord.
[2]* The Abels.
[3]* Virginity stands for faithfulness

9

He goes; they have been redeemed from amongst men to be the first-fruits for God and for the Lamb; they never allowed a lie to pass their lips and no fault can be found in them." [1] "they are the learned who supply to My lambs truthfulness and who shine as brightly as the vault of heaven, and as bright as stars for all eternity;" [2] those who produce the fruit of disobedience are a living abomination

[1] Ap. 14 : 4-5
[2] Dn 12 : 3

10

in My Eyes and a condemnation of the way they disobey the Law given by My Church .... alas, for that Day! alas, for My Day, which is drawing near, it will be a day of great sorrow that day; for the unlawful it will be terror, since they had put Me, their Lord, to the test; but I tell you, the supporters of the Beast will fall together with their pride and power and everything they have will crumble into dust; why have they not listened

11

to Me when I said this parable to the people? the parable of the wicked husbandmen;*[1] the scribes and the chief priests who were there listening to Me, got annoyed at once and if it were not that they feared the people, they would have laid their hands on Me; today still I have tenants who are in My Vineyard*[2] who act like the wicked husbandmen towards those I am sending to them, not only do they mistreat

*[1] Lk 20 : 9-19 *[2] The Church

12

them but they would be ready to sell My Blood too;* O what sorrow, daughter what agony to see them pose as men devoted to My Law, but I, who read in their heart, know the contents of their heart ... have they looked who is standing outside their door knocking? and yet whom they allowed to sit at table next to them and share their meal? they allowed those evil forces to dine with them and sit side by side at table

* Jesus means, abolish His Perpetual Sacrifice

13

with them, have they not read: "it was the stone rejected by the builders that became the keystone"; with this, I tell you* again, that the day you will fall on that stone you will be dashed to pieces; anyone it falls on will be crushed; and you, daughter of My Church, even if the evil powers and all hell are working through them against you, it is because they realized you are a danger to them and that My Messages regarding the

* Followers of the Beast.

14

Beast of John's Revelation*[1] are aimed at them; yes, you have become a menace to all these dark powers and Satan will go as far as to put even nature against you; this powerful enemy is at your heels*[2] but do not fear, My Holy Spirit living in you is far greater and much more powerful than all hell put together; so, go and fill all the nations with My Words; let Me remind you, dearest soul, that I have

*[1] Ap. 13. *[2] It means, running after me.

15

brought you up to tear up iniquity and unsettle and upset every evil spirit you encounter on your way or in the cities you go to witness, so do not be surprised when these powers of hell join forces together to try and prevent you from exercising your prophetic ministry; these attacks are bound to come your way as soon as they realize you are well on your way to disturb them and uproot many of them; you have indeed become a menace and the prime

16

concern to the devil because you do not only carry My Word, which is holy and sanctifies you, but also the power of My Holy Spirit who lives in you terrifies them, because My Holy Spirit gives the world the utter conviction that you come from Me, the Christ.... I have also brought you up to help build up the ruins of My Sanctuary and to plant in this desert ♡ so do not fear, 'lo tedhal',* I have already

* In His own language, Aramaic, 'do not fear.'

promised you that we shall finish your mission hand in hand with success and with victory; I have formed you strong, to be able to face this powerful enemy; I have given you the Spirit of Fortitilde so that you proclaim My Word and My Tradition thrice blessed, to the utmost capacity, and the power that graciously descends from My Spirit will give you utterance; My Spirit will be your strength so that you carry the crosses with courage till the end; so let My Word

18

strike through you <u>and</u> pierce all the kingdoms of the world, dragging them all down to destruction; yes! I shall continue to use you against those evil powers through My Spirit of Fortitude and even, in this battle, when from time to time, you will be drenched with blood by their vicious attacks, My Mother and I will uphold you; the destructive scourge would not catch you; I, the Christ, will walk before you, so that with My Sceptre I may

19

point out to you the traitors of My Church who need your prayers; I will encourage you to pursue the sinners the great and the proud, the hypocrites, the rebels and the lofty speakers; with My Cross in one hand and the rosary in the other, you are to shatter the heresies and build Truth and Faithfulness in their place ♡ I will continue to set you at large so that you may crown Me with your fruit; *O slaves of the

* Then Jesus turned to cry out after the followers of the Beast.

20

Beast! can you not see how he*[1] is leading you slowly and slyly to your destruction?*[2] but, plot though you do to harm My Church and weave your plan as you may, you cannot and will not triumph, I will be triumphant in the end; I have already unmasked to the nations part of your plan, and the day the Rebel will appear", that day you*[3] appear, I will unmask to

*[1] The Beast
*[2] I felt Jesus' pain and how in spite of their faults He loved them dearly. *[3] Jesus speaks to the Rebel.

the nations your entire plan of destruction; I will reveal to the entire world the intentions of your heart...." go now and remind My children, that I am their Rock and I will never fail them; I have solemnly warned them previously and I will persistently keep warning them ♡ remain always faithful to Me and to the Tradition of the Church, remain faithful to the Institution of My Eucharist, recognizing Me in My Body ♡ remain faithful to the teachings of this Pope

22

which are sound because they are founded in the Truth; I am the Truth; My little children, do not stray away from the Truth, remain in the Truth; by remaining in the Truth you will remain in Me;

Your Eyes, my Lord, are turned on the sinful kingdoms of the world to wipe away each one of them from the surface of the earth, but will there be forgiveness to those who were tempted?

if they will repent, acknowledging their sin, and swear loyalty in front of

23

My Throne, I will remember the oath that they made with Me when they were ordained and I will pardon them with all My Heart ♡ come, do not forget to pray for these souls .... come, in your persecutions, My Father in heaven, blesses you, to remain firm; in your hardships, I am by your side to sustain you; in times of danger*, My Holy Spirit is your Guide and your Protector; so

* I understood it as 'times of temptations'.

24

proclaim My Message with faith and courage; I am a gentle God who loves you, and remember, consolation is to be found in Me! ic

ΙΧΘΥΣ 

1. 11. 96

My Saviour, I give thanks to
Your Holy Name,
for Your Love and Your marvels;
but see, sometimes my courage
runs low, and in my
misery, misery because of my own
guilt, I feel things are
raising like a gale that comes
Lashing up on me like
towering waves; and I cry out:
" Oh, what to do? "
And not until the waves grow quiet

again, could my soul savour Peace....

fear not, endeavour to please Me; withhold Me not from being with you in this way too, just you and Me.... be My pilgrim, the pilgrim of My Heart and remain in My Heart forever; I guarantee to you that your soul will enjoy the delights of My Sacred Heart; My Lips will keep feeding you and My Heart will keep loving you and consoling you; every step you will take I will be taken with Me,

26

your Saviour; are you happy now that you are with Me in this way, daughter of My Heart?

Lord, to this very day, after all these years of being in conversation with You, I am still dazed and uncomprehending of Your choice! Here I was, a corpse without honour and who comes to visit me? The Invincible One, the Most High! And You ask me now whether I am happy to be with You?

yes, I have, daughter*....

I have never deserved all this, and I cannot express any thought that

* Here I was amazed at Christ's simplicity and the way He said it, like a child.

is worthy of Your Gift, since You Yourself are this Gift; You are my joy, my peace, my incense, my smile, my laughter, You are my delight, my life, my breath, the light of my eyes, You are my father, my mother, my child, my friend, You are my Lord and my God! You are the radiance of my soul, and there is no one to compare You with, so yes, I am dying of happiness when I am with You!

yes! love Me and prefer Me to anything and anybody; in My company all good things will come to you. My friend, and My sister,* would it be too much if I asked you another

* I think Christ made a point to call me 'sister', since I did not tell Him that He is my Brother too.

28

question?

No, my Lord;

Vassula, is My Law your delight?

O yes! Your Law is Yourself, Your whole Being and all that You are; Your Law, my Saviour, is Life for me.

I have heard My Spirit speak through your mouth, for this you are My delight too ♡ let the people know how I lift souls to Me with My Love.... now, listen Vassula and answer Me sincerely this last question: in

29

the end I will triumph, but, meanwhile, I have to suffer and endure all the triumphs of Satan; I call them triumphs every time he manages to bring to damnation a soul; My question to you is: "will you delight Me, your God and be like a lily?"

What can a mere lily do for You? *

a lily does not worry about tomorrow; each day has enough worries of its own; can you, for all your worrying

* *I was surprised by His question.*

30

change anything on your own? follow My programs I laid out for you and trust Me entirely! so, do you want to be like a lily?

If this is what pleases You, yes.

forget yourself in My Arms; die to yourself and renounce yourself so that you can take up My Cross together with Me; attach yourself to My Cross and together, I and you, will share It for the salvation of souls; through My Cross I triumphed

31

and will triumph again this time over Satan's plans; be one with Me and allow yourself to be carried by Me; I, Jesus, bless you; ic

New York* 8. 11. 96

(5.00 p.m)

My Lord?

I Am; every minute of your life I am with you; My Hand is with you, so rejoice and be glad and blessed;

*First meeting on this journey which follows: Tampa, Florida, Charleston, Atlanta, Washington DC., Indianapolis, Minneapolis, St. Louis.

32

before you begin;* tell My children that I bless each one of them and that My Peace I give to them; tell them also that the Father and I rejoice in them every time they invoke Our Name with love; so now declare to the world all that you have learnt from Us; God-is-with-you

Florida- Tampa 9. 11. 9

Lord?

I Am, I shall never fail you, never!

* Jesus means, 'begin witnessing in the conference

My Love for them is beyond human understanding and today I descend from above to be in a very special way with them; come and grow in My Love so that your union with Me may be perfected; when the first-fruits are made holy so is the whole batch*; you are My first-fruits and I want you holy!.... so come! confess your sins often so that the devil will not

* That means that from their conversions they could draw others to conversion.

34

be given a foot-hold .... I bless each one of you; be one! ic

S. Carolina - Charleston 10.11.96

peace be with you; in times of crisis I intervened; I am known for My Mercy; today I am offering you again My Sacred Heart and I tell you:

anyone of you who turns to Me with the sole desire to please Me, with all My Heart, yes, with all My Heart I will grant them My favours .... I will reveal the Treasures of My Heart to

35

them so that they end their journey with Me ... Love is with you; ic

St. Louis 17.11.96

My Lord, You who are Wisdom,
You who are Life and Light within us,
I praise Your Name Thrice Holy;
Let all Goodness seduce my soul
so that I may live in Your reflection;

Omnipresence! Joy and Peace of my heart,
Your Presence leaves me tranquil
and Your Uprightness sparks a flame within me,
to show me that I am the offspring
of the Goodness of my soul;

Glory be to our Lord Thrice Holy,
Alleluia!

36

My loved one, My Sacred Heart quivers with emotion; how I longed to hear My offspring say to Me one day these words! from all eternity your words were written in My Sacred Heart and I waited patiently, oh, ever so patiently for you to pronounce them! enjoy now My Presence and drink from Me, eat from Me ..... I have not laboured in vain in you to raise you up; enjoy these Inexhaustible riches that I had reserved for your times now

37

and show them to the world, this world that has grown cold and is dead to love; show My Inexhaustible Treasure to every nation and tell them that greater gift than My Sacred Heart they could not receive;

and you, My remnant, bless My children for Me; those who accompanied you, since they have dedicated their time for Me;* yes! My Heart is touched to tears; I love you, I love you with all My Heart.... ic

* Jesus again quivered with emotion.

38

27. 11. 96

peace be with you; you have said well to My people that all goodness comes from Me; only God is good and I supply My goodness to every creature, I fill their reserves so that they do not lack; rich are My depths and rich is My generosity; Vassula, My cheerful messenger, grafted on to Me, receive My Holy Spirit and do not be afraid; I say to you, do not fear the world, this world that has turned pagan from their apostasy, but since I am Lord both of the dead and of the living, My aim is to resurrect the dead; My aim is to renew My Church and I put this duty to you, a duty beyond your means and your capacity, but do not forget who is with you; I am with you and I am Strength and Power; no one can say that all that has been achieved to this day came from you; in one's nothingness you expect nothing, I chose an ignorant child so that all the undertakings will be done by Me; so, go in

40

My Name, go forward and proclaim My Messages which are a healing balm to mankind; do not be discouraged when from time to time the current opposes you, hold on to Me, stand firm when trials come your way, in the fight against apostasy, you have not yet had to fight alone, remember I am with you.... and I know those who are My Own. My Heart grieves continuously to watch those in My House who lack sincerity and who do not work in My Spirit for

41

the unification of the dates of Easter; I ask you to pray for them that My Father may give them a change of mind so that once their eyes are opened by My Holy Spirit, they will repent and recognize their error which prevented them from seeing the Truth; pray for them that this spirit of pride in them, keeping them separated from the Truth, leaves them and brings them back to their senses; pray for them so that I may be able to say: " by their love, all men now will

42

know that they are truly My disciples;" but today still, Satan and his demons keep them chained in their lack of love, for love is the distinctive sign of faith; how could they say to one another: "I have preached the Good News throughout the world; I have laboured to bring the Church into one and now all there is to come is the crown of righteousness which the Lord, my God, reserved for me from all eternity..." when to this very day they are failing in their duty?

43

all priests should imitate Me in their life; I am not speaking of those who imitate Me and are like My Abel who was pleasing to Us, because of his sacrifices and his sincerity, but of those who are like Cain, and Essau and Juda and the Scribes and the Pharisees; of these I am speaking, for their conduct contradicts My Holy Rules; must I, for their sake, go on drinking from the cup of your division, this cup forced on Me by them? so far I have put no pressure*

* by chastisement

44

on you*, I have been pleading with you to unify the dates of Easter but you are not hearing My Spirit; you have exploited the patience of My Father; this time again I am asking you to unite the Easter dates so that My Spirit shines on you with grace and brings My House into one; today I am speaking to you but you do not value My words in these Messages; when you will one day, it will be too late ... ah! if only one

* Christ speaks to them.

45

of these men working for unity, if only one of them does not give in to his passions, to his fears, and goes forward unifying the dates of Easter, I, God, will exalt him; — but what I see from the House of the East are tempers roused, obstinacies and fears, brothers yet adversaries; House of the East you have done well in maintaining the Tradition as I passed It on to you and as My primitive church exercised It, however, you are not allowing My Holy Spirit to nurture

46

you enough for your salvation and the salvation of those who are in desperate need of salvation .... you harass My first-fruits*, and My messengers, rejecting them together with My Holy Spirit of grace who brought them to walk in His path; and you continue to expel them from My Sanctuaries as I too was by the high priests of My time.... in the meantime My flock is dispersed and the loss of souls increases daily; so I tell you, come,

* The newly converted from 'True Life in God'

be ambitious for the gifts of My Spirit and do not leave My House barren; My House will benefit from My Spirit's gifts if you open the door of your heart....

and you, House of the West, you have realized, through the Light of My Spirit, that a body needs its two lungs to breathe freely, and that My Body is imperfect with one lung; pray that My vivifying Spirit will join you together, but what have I to suffer before! *

* I understood at the same time: "What have <u>we</u> to suffer before!" The "we" was meant for Pope John Paul II together with Jesus.

48

the world transgresses and rejects My Commandments and Satan wants to destroy what I had instituted, he wants to destroy what I, the Lamb, left you with: My Church; he puts her in confusion, disorder and My Body is torn asunder by a spirit of rebellion, a rationalistic and naturalistic spirit has populated My Body, who disown Me in the Blessed Sacrament; of these, very few are concerned for My Interests, and so many are trampling upon My Laws as if

49

they were not given by God! there is an antagonistic spirit hovering over My Church, but not for long now.... so I implore you, House of the West, to go forward and unmask the Evil one by unifying the dates of Easter as in the primitive Church; anyone who wants to become great among you must be your servant, and anyone who wants to be first among you must be slave to all; My primitive Church was like a child, innocent,

50

and full of love because she was carried in the Arms of My Holy Spirit, then I heard: "I am not a child any longer and I can walk now by myself;" and since then she stepped out of My Holy Spirit's embrace and accustomed her steps to walk her own way....

O child of the Father! My fruit! city and bride of My Holy Spirit, your fragrance left you.... so come back to Me as a child and My grace will be upon you and My Holy Spirit thrice

51

Holy will be your guide and your lamp; for this I need intense poverty of the spirit and an overflow of generosity, ah... but children are poor in spirit and generous too because Wisdom lives in them and is their guide too ♡

Eve of the 11th anniversary 27. 11. 96
of True Life in God.

By Your Word my God You raised me to sing to me and to all my brothers and sisters this new song of Love;

My bones were wasting away and my heart had grown parched and had become a land of drought; ruin had crept on me

in my total unawareness,
I was empty and hungry and I lacked,
I was filled with everything
but Goodness;

Marvel of Love,
You came in my night, You came to
the one who had ceased to be,
to fill me by the Breath of Your Mouth.
and bring me to be;

And now I can say:
I have been raised in the Courts of
my Father and my flesh
bloomed again and my heart
breathes and longs for my God,
thrice Holy, all day long;

God, my Saviour, You know that
I am not worthy to walk in Your
Sacred Courts, but I love Your
House, I love the House where You live;
I am not worthy to walk around

53

Your Throne and to gaze my
fill on Your likeness;

Lord, Let Your creation feast on Your
Riches, give them Rivers to drink,
give them abundant Manna to eat;
With You, my Lord, is the
Fountain of Life, with You, my Lord,
is the Tree of Life, so come,
Come in our darkness,
come by Your Light so that
we see Your Light;

Lord, my God, hear me and
side with me,
Come and renew Your creation,
so that nothing can ever
shake us again!

Glory be to God, the God of Glory,
my life, I give to You;

Amen.

54

peace be with you; your petitions reached Me .... *[1] can the dust do anything ♡ by itself? *[2] see?

yet You heard my petitions. You must have heard and felt my heart which longs for You.

My delight and My child, be strong against all evil forces, remain in My favour and look after My Interests; be My Echo .... display My Holiness to the world, display the Riches of

*[1] There was silence and I wondered for a brief moment whether He had gone.

*[2] He just wanted to prove to me that it is by the Power of the Holy Spirit that I can hear Him.

55

My Sacred Heart to every nation;* have you not noticed that I have given My orders to the skies above to open the doors of heaven and rain down Rivers together with Manna? I want to nourish you all with My Word; Vassula, the simple of heart find Me and possess Me but there are thousands out there in the desert who are naked and starved and although they see

* By this, Christ means, to every body, not only to Catholics but to all!

themselves covered with rich vestments, in reality they are naked, starved and pitiable to look at; although they are starving for lack of My Word, they believe they are feasting; there is no time to spare, My child; this is why I am sending you in My Name to tell them that the Lord has prepared for them a banquet ....

ΙΧΘΥΣ

57

11th Anniversary of True Life in God
28.11.96

Blessed be my Rock,
Blessed be my Saviour,
Blessed be His Sacred Heart,
this Heart that displays its
Love for all mankind,
This Heart which is more desirable
than the finest gold, because the
treasures* it contains are
sweeter than honey;

Blessed be His Sacred Heart,
this Heart that lifted me
and formed me,
O Lord, come and display to
mankind Your marvels, come
and display Your marvellous kindness!

I will never fail you; My Sacred
Heart was offered to you so that It

* 'treasures' stand for: 'the Words of God.'

58

becomes the sunshine of your soul, the delight of your heart and the joy of your life; My desire was to revive you and hear you .... caress Me with your love; your thirst for Me is a soothing balm on My wounded Heart .... come!, allow Me to pour through you a spirit of kindness and prayer so that I remind the world of My marvels and the power of My Mercy in My loving kindness; My Heart is inflamed with love for all mankind and

59

the more they will advance reading Me the more sanctifying graces will I be pouring on them, to draw them deeper into the flames of My Heart; — I am infinitely rich in grace and I want to draw them into this* Heart, this Heart that delights to be with the sons and daughters of men; in My Sacred Heart are riches and honour, lasting wealth and loyalty; My Treasures will make you walk in the path of virtue; happy the eyes that see what they see in My Heart,

* He pointed to His Heart

60

and obtain it, he will obtain life and he will win My Father's favour, and We will be by his side, delighting him day after day, pouring blessing after blessing on him and on his whole household; My Sacred Heart is like an appeasing fragrance, It is like the sun shining in your obscurity; My Sacred Heart is sweeter than honey and I welcome all mouths to taste My sweetness; My Sacred Heart is like a bed of selected roses; My Sacred Heart is filled with graciousness;

61

yes, It is like a wellspring of life; turn your eyes on My Sacred Heart and Its brightness will fill your dark night into the fullness of day; hold My Sacred Heart and embrace It and Its closeness to you will set a crown of sanctifying grace on your head, which will bring your feet into the path of loyalty, even to accept shedding your blood for My honour; the Invincible holiness of My Sacred Heart can be your shield when evil is glorified by

62

evil; My Sacred Heart is like a tree filled with fruit, with rich foliage in which you can take shelter beneath Its branches; the fire from My Heart is the power to give you light in your soul, not even the most blazing stars could ever illuminate the dreadful night of your soul as the fire coming from within My Heart, indeed, the fire of My Sacred Heart is a thousand times more resplendant than the sun; it is like putting a thousand times more than all the constellations of the

63

universe together; with Me are divine love, divine mercy, divine fruit, divine light, divine sweetness, divine springs, divine wealth, enriching those who approach Me filling their treasuries with My purity; anxious to save My people from death, I said: "I shall come to them with My Heart in My Hand and open My Heart like a reservoir and immerse them with My divine Treasures; I will come upon them like a huge ocean, to fortify them;

64

with what can you compare My Heart, this Heart that laid down the Foundations of My Sanctuary? like a sprig of frankincense in summer-time? like the melody of a harp? like some jewel of crystal-clear diamond? nothing can be compared to the invincible holiness of My Sacred Heart, for within My Heart are sanctifying graces, because It is unique in Its splendour, manifold in Its graces and virtues, subtle, gentle and compassionate

Excerpts from Notebook 87

28 November 96, continued from Notebook #86, p.64...Since My Heart is the throne of grace, have confidence in My benevolence

- ✠ Know that you have a permanent place in My Sacred Heart
- ✠ Divine and irresistible is My Sacred Heart, for it holds all the riches of your salvation
- ✠ So many of My children...abandon and scorn this merciful Heart
- ✠ When your eyes will contemplate in your misery the majesty of My Heart, your soul will be overcome with an incessant longing for My rulings...My decrees will become your delight and your counsellors
- ✠ Happy the man who discovers the steadfastness of My Sacred Heart...beyond the price of pearls
- ✠ Vassula, I have come again to revive the devotion to My Sacred Heart
- ✠ Have you not read that a Fountain will spring from the House of Yahweh?...like cascades this living water will pour out of My Heart
- ✠ I have come to you, puny little creature, to show the world the Power of My Sacred Heart and My Infinite Mercy...I have charged you with a task far beyond your means
- ✠ I will let this Fountain...invade this cold world, giving life wherever It will pass
- ✠ I had given...to My beloved disciple John, a glimpse of My Treasures in My Heart that led him, in the terrors of that day, all the way to My Cross...later on he invited Gertrude to revere My Sacred Heart...her eyes rained tears of joy
- ✠ <u>The real knowledge is to know Us, in Our Trinitarian Holiness</u> and live in an intimate union with us...so let the devotion of My Sacred Heart be known to all people
- ✠ Tell them that whosoever practices this devotion...will obtain sanctifying graces...for all their household

even to the most wretched among you; My Heart is active because I am the Word and the Word of God is something alive and active; My Heart is invulnerable in Its Glory!; It is benevolent and full of mercy when you are in need of help; since My Heart is the throne of grace, have confidence in My benevolence, I sympathize with your ignorance, do not lose courage; know that you have a permanent place in My Sacred Heart; I am the Word of God

2

and from My Mouth comes an incisive sword; I am here, and My Heart will undertake all things that are not right and put them right with My sword; My Sacred Heart is not complicated, I am not a complicated God, because I am like a lamp, shining from within and from without, and completely lucid, therefore, you will never be misled, and I will reassure you all the time that holiness will be rewarded in the end; My Sacred Heart is so lucid and pure, It is the Light of the world, divine and irresistible is My Sacred Heart, for It holds all the riches of your salvation; it is he who receives this Heart graciously that will be acknowleding Us as thrice Holy with reverence, faithfulness and honour,

and in My divinity I will lead him into eternal life ♡ My Sacred Heart, throbs with love for mankind because It is loving to man; if you approach Me like a child, I will place My Sacred Heart in the palm of your hand and

4

when you will see My Treasures, with learned sayings revealling My mysteries and My secrets, your holy fear for Me will seize you because you will realize that I am God, triune but One in the unity of essence, dearer to you than all the wealth of the world and even your own life; ah Vassula .... mercy is to be found with Me, yet so many of My children abandon and scorn this mercifull Heart; exile though you are on earth, creation,

5

open your eyes to contemplate My Sacred Heart, open your eyes and your heart to the marvels engraved in My Heart; I will not hide My inestimable Treasures from you; although you are an exile, I shall open the door of My Heart and when your eyes will contemplate in your misery the majesty of My Heart, your soul will be overcome with an incessant longing for My rulings, and My decrees will become your delight and your

6

counsellors, then you will voluntarily ask Me to become the victim of the Victim, the crucifix of the Crucified and you will proclaim My decrees to the world, without fear of disgrace, remembering Who had found you, an exile, in the exile ♡; then you will say to Me, showing Me My Sacred Heart: "Master, here I will stay for ever, this is the home I have chosen ♡" faithfulness is the essence of My Word, and I am known to

7

be faithful and true; there is no deceit in My Heart, My Sacred Heart is your heaven, filled with righteous rulings; happy the man who discovers the steadfastness of My Sacred Heart which is beyond the price of pearls; nothing you could covet is its equal;

My sons, My daughters, there is nothing equal to My Sacred Heart, for I am the Alpha and the Omega; and the ways of My Sacred Heart are delightful ways, leading into the

8

intimacy so desired by Us*[1]; to what can you compare My Sacred Heart? to a Fountain that makes the gardens fertile? yes, so if any man is thirsty, let him come to Me! let the man come and drink; My Heart is a well of living water; come and immerse yourself in those streams*[2] that flow out from My Sacred Heart; My Sacred Heart is your guarantor and the Tree of Life for those who will possess It ♡

*[1] The Trinity.
*[2] Jesus was speaking about His Spirit.

9

do not let your feet take you down to death; learn that My tender Sacred Heart is glorious and majestic, dependable, faithful and true; It is framed in steadfastness, transcending the heavens; It raises, Vassula, the poor from dust* and out of their misery, to give them a place in Its depths, in the depths of Infinite Mercy; let My Sacred Heart be the Root that supports you and you, you have been grafted on to Me

* Jesus was hinting this for me; the way He raised me & gave me a place in His Heart.

10

to share My rich sap that provides you with life, eternal life; so remain grafted on Me to be part of Me and your life will be spared; Vassula, I have come again to revive the devotion to My Sacred Heart, happy all those who follow this devotion; the world, is dead to love because it has distanced itself from Us*, and by forsaking the Fountain of Wisdom, it died in its drought; this is why I have come, with My Heart in My Hand, to

* The Trinity

11

you so you feel the pulsations of My Heart; do not be surprised, have you not read that a Fountain will spring from the House of Yahweh*[1]? and like cascades this living water*[2] will pour out of My Heart.... yes, so that all of you gain freedom, this freedom that is solely found in My Spirit ♡ I have come to you, not because of your merits, since you had none, I have not only chosen you because of your wretchedness

*[1] Joel 4:18 *[2] Holy Spirit

12

and your nothingness, as you tell people, but it was also because of your insignificance and your total ignorance in all matters that concerned My Sacred Heart, yes! *and My Church too; drenched in sin and not virtue, portrait of your society and far from My Own traits, you were appalling even in My Angels' eyes! yet, I have come to you, puny little creature, to show the world the Power of My Sacred

* I thought, of the Church too...

13

Heart and My Infinite Mercy, I have come in your ignorance and charged you with a task far beyond your means and I have made My Sacred Heart known to you and I will continue to make It known in this cold world drenched in its blood from its crimes; I will let this Fountain* from My Sacred Heart invade this cold world, giving life wherever It will pass and My Promise will be accomplished because My Holy Spirit, the Giver of

* Jesus speaks about His Holy Spirit

14

Life will govern this wicked society and turn it into an upright people, then holiness and justice will be their consort; Vassula, I had given, in the past, to My beloved disciple John, a glimpse of My Treasures in My Heart, that led him, in the terrors of that day, all the way to My Cross; then, later on, he invited Gertrude to revere My Sacred Heart, showing her the value of the Treasures hidden in My Heart; her eyes rained tears of joy when she

15

saw those divine Treasures, I have been longing to reveal to you in your day and age the Riches of a mystery kept secret for endless ages; so honour My Sacred Heart and be innocent, be the salt of the earth and the light, so that you will shine in the world like a bright star, because you will be offering it* the Word of Life; fall on your knees now and praise Me! see how mighty are My wonders? see how great

* the world

16

are My marvels? let My Yoke be light on you and not burden you and you will have no trace of fatigue.... pursue the path I have traced for you and tell My people that no one can survive with his intellect only, and I never reveal Myself to those who claim to have knowledge only of earthly things, for this is not the real knowledge that comes from God; the real knowledge is to know Us, in Our Trinitarian Holiness and live in an intimate

17

union with Us, I have no favourites, so let the devotion of My Sacred Heart be known to all people[1]; be one in Us; We love you, dear child ♡ receive Our blessings;   IXΘYΣ

Later:

yes! this[2] was given to you on the eleventh anniversary of My saving Message; I will continue to fill your mouth and nourish you with My Word; you will continue to obtain from My Heart abundant

[1] Jesus means not only to Catholics but all others too.
[2] The Message above.

sanctifying graces to accomplish your mission; and as I said to My other apostles of My Sacred Heart, I also tell you: love this Heart that is so unloved, revive My devotion of My Sacred Heart and tell them* that whosoever practices this devotion, they will obtain sanctifying graces not only for themselves but also for all their household;" and you, My loved one, be one with Me; ic

* To the people

Prayers Given to Vassula

Jesus to Vassula
January 29, 1990

Lord my God,
lift my soul from this darkness
into Your Light,
envelop my soul into Your
Sacred Heart,
feed my soul with Your Word,
anoint my soul
with Your Holy Name,
make my soul ready to
hear Your discourse,
breathe Your sweet fragrance
on my soul, reviving it,
ravish my soul
to delight Your Soul,
Father, embellish me, Your child,
by distilling Your pure myrrh
upon me,

You have taken me to Your
Celestial Hall,
where all the Elect are seated,
You have shown me around
to Your angels, ah,
what more does my soul ask?

Your Spirit has given me life
and You, who are the living
Bread have restored my life,
You have offered me to drink
Your Blood,
to be able to share for eternity
with You, Your Kingdom
and live forever and ever,

Glory be to the Highest!
Glory be to the Holy of Holies.
Praised be Our Lord.
Blessed be Our Lord, for His
Mercy and His Love
reaches from age to age
and forever will;
Amen.

Mary to Vassula
May 15, 1990

Father all Merciful,
let those who hear and hear again
yet never understand,
hear Your Voice this time and
understand that it is You
the Holy of Holies;
open the eyes of those who see
and see, yet never perceive, to
see with their eyes this time
Your Holy Face and Your Glory,
place Your Finger on their heart
so that their heart may open and
understand Your Faithfulness,

I pray and ask you all these
things Righteous Father,
so that all the nation be
converted and be healed through
the Wounds of Your Beloved Son,
Jesus Christ; Amen.

Prayers Jesus Recommended to Vassula
(to be said daily)

Novena of Confidence to the Sacred Heart

O Lord, Jesus Christ,
to Your Most Sacred Heart
I confide this intention (state
your request).

Only look upon me,
then do what Your Heart
inspires,
Let Your Sacred Heart decide,
I count on It, I trust in It,
I throw myself on Its Mercy.

Lord Jesus, You will not fail me.
Sacred Heart of Jesus,
I trust in Thee.
Sacred Heart of Jesus,
I believe in Thy love for me.
Sacred Heart of Jesus,
Thy Kingdom come.

O Sacred Heart of Jesus,
I have asked for many favors,
but I earnestly implore this one.
Take it. Place it in Thy Sacred
Heart.
When the Eternal Father sees it
covered with Thy Precious
Blood,
He will not refuse it.
It will be no longer my prayer,
but Thine, O Jesus.

O Sacred Heart of Jesus,
I place my trust in Thee.
Let me never be confounded.
Amen.

Prayer to St. Michael

St. Michael, the archangel,
defend us in the day of battle;
be our safeguard against the
wickedness and snares of the
devil.

May God rebuke him, we
humbly pray, and do thou,
O prince of the heavenly host,
by the power of God, cast into
hell, Satan, and all the other evil
spirits, who prowl through the
world seeking the ruin of souls.
Amen.

The Memorare of St. Bernard

Remember, O most gracious
Virgin Mary, that never was
it known that anyone who fled
to your protection, implored
your help, or sought your
intercession, was left unaided.

Inspired with this confidence,
I fly unto you.
O Virgin of Virgins,
my Mother!
To you I come, before you
I stand sinful and sorrowful.
O Mother of the Word
Incarnate, despise not my
petitions, but in your mercy,
hear and answer me.
Amen.